PRAISE FOR THE BUSINESS OWNERS COMPENDIUM

"The compendium is a super useful guide that I will be referring all of my clients to use. One of the things I most appreciated was how comprehensive it is without being overwhelming. It gave me just the right amount of information to take action and outside resources if I wanted to explore more. It helped me do a review of my business practices but I would suggest it for any new business owner or anyone interested in re-organizing/restructuring their business"

Kelly Sheets

Kelly Sheets.com

"Solari's book - The Business Owner's Compendium - *A practical guide to the theory of starting, owning, and operating a business, should be required reading for anyone wanting to start their own business. Most other books on starting your own business tell you "why" to start a business… this book shows you "how" to successfully start and run a business! It offers successful and useful advice and acumen from someone who truly understands the business of of starting and running a business!"*

Doug Dvorak

Founder & Managing Principal - The Digital Marketing Group, Inc.

"Big business analysis for small business owners. Joe brings his sophistication with numbers to small business entrepreneurs looking to start or grow. He makes a great case for buying a business, too. Joe looks at the big trends in small business and distills them to actionable steps. Keep this guide close."

John Heintz

Second Rail Education

John wakes up every day strategizing. He helps idea people execute on their goals in the international education, law and management.

"An indispensable set of advice and tools for anyone who operates or is thinking of launching their own business."

Ray Berardinelli,

RB Marketing Communications

BUSINESS OWNER'S COMPENDIUM

A PRACTICAL GUIDE TO THE THEORY OF STARTING, OWNING, AND OPERATING A BUSINESS

JOE SOLARI

CLAYMORE ULFBERHT & XIPHOS LLC

I dedicate this book to my lovely wife Suze and my wonderful son's Rowan and Vincent.

Cover design by 100covers
Edited by tessywriter
Copyright 2017 by Claymore Ulfberht & Xiphos LLC
All rights reserved
Ebook ASIN B0728G3T7N
Print ISBN 9781521430170

Please Contact the Author at Hi@middle-marketplace.com for permission to use the copyright material.

Purchasers of the book have the rights to use the worksheets and files provided in conjunction with the book for their personal use and for use in their business.

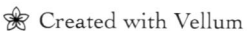 Created with Vellum

CONTENTS

Is this book for you?	ix
Acknowledgments	xvii
caveat, disclaimer, safe harbor disclosure	xix
Introduction	xxi

PART ONE
GETTING STARTED

Being Your Own Boss	3
Risk & Return	5
Business Demographics	26
Ownership	32
Incorporation	69

PART TWO
RUNNING A BUSINESS

Financial Command	91
Financing Your Business	147
Ratios you Should Know	184
Productivity and Automation	192
Marketing	201
Sales	223
Inventory and Pricing	235
Planning and Time Management	250
Taxes	269
Financial Modeling	272
What Now?	284

Bibliography	287
Affiliate Links	289
Current List of Files and Worksheets	291
Afterword	293
About the Author	295

IS THIS BOOK FOR YOU?

Is This Book for You?

Let me help you with the decision you face about buying this book. If you are like me, you use the "look inside" feature to evaluate if a book has any value. How frustrating when there is no meaningful content in the sample—only titles, dedications, and blurbs. In the spirit and style of the book, here is the distillation of the book for your evaluation:

Target Audience:

- Small business owners
- Self-employed freelancers, consultants, authors, and other businesses with only an owner/employee—this would include the newly minted term of solopreneurs entrepreneurs with no intention of having employees
- Home based business operators
- A person who has a hobby business ready to transition from working a day job to self-employment
- Someone who is doing research to start their own small business

Who is this book not for?

This is not a guide on Tech Start-ups, or how to get to your idea to a minimum viable product. While tech start-ups will face the issues, I discuss and benefit from the tools herein, if you're looking for help in early tech start-up issues, this is likely not the book for you.

Controlling Idea:

Every business owner faces a point where what they do next will determine if the business works for them or they will work for the business. Regardless of success or failure, the number of employees, how big or small your business is now or will be in the future, you must be purposeful it the design and operation of your business. If you do not, you will not control your business; the business will control you.

Structure:

Each section is designed to get you making effective change in your business; some theory so you understand why, and then actionable processes and tools to get results.

Don't feel that you need to read this book from front to back but go to the sections where you feel the most pain and start work. The most effective way to get improvement is to focus on the biggest problem and correct that one thing.

Resources:

Throughout the book, there are resources referenced. They include swipe files, checklists, spreadsheets, models, and simulators. Any of these tools I reference will be supplied as links in the book, and you will have free access with the purchase of the book to dozens of these tools to download from a website. The tools are designed to expedite your planning or problem-solving.

Objectives:

A. Help the owners of small businesses align the business with their purpose and provide tools that keep them from becoming servants to their business.

B. Provide tools and know-how to freelancers and other self-employed individuals to scale a business.

C. Educate those exploring a start-up on the right processes to put in place to avoid the common pitfalls of a new business.

D. Inform the reader about how to think about risk and reward and how the correct mindset with the right tools can help harden your business to adversity and provide the owner with an appropriate return.

Questions to confirm if this book is for you

If you answer yes to just one of these questions, this book is for you!

You want to do your own thing but you're not sure how much time or cash will be needed?

You have concerns about having or getting the capital needed to fund your business idea?

You need to raise money to expand your business?

Do you own a home-based business and are finding the business is getting more complex?

Do you struggle with and planning?

Are you an owner of small businesses that is looking for a resource guide to help systematize your business?

Do you lack confidence around the finances of your business?

Have you started a business in support of your passion or purpose and look to fill in your knowledge gaps?

Have you recognized that demands on your time and attention are drawing you away from why you started the business in the first place?

Are you an architect passionate about your vision, an artist looking to sell your work, an engineer solving an industry problem, an independent truck driver, or self-employed running a retail operation?

No matter what you set out to do, one day, it came to you —

"Oh, S%*T! I have a business now,"

followed by

"and it's getting away from me."

If you answered yes to any of the above questions then you will find what you need in this book.

You are not alone. This is the most common issue that faces business owners as they grow an enterprise. I know this because for the several years I have been interviewing small business owners about what is keeping them up at night. Eventually, we get back to priority and, more importantly, not having the time to do what they believe is fun and important.

I will show ways to get back to what matters and get you spending your time on where you and your business will get the most benefit. There are actionable processes in this book that will, if followed, get you back on the track of purposeful work.

This book may also be helpful if you are planning to start a business and are trying to thwart the usual pitfalls of small businesses.

I wanted to provide one place where you could go to get help quickly—something akin to a recipe book—to help you whip up solutions to the common business problems. When you identify an issue, you go to this book and find some practical methods and tools to find out what is causing you to get off course, then correct the course, finally putting in place processes that keep you on course.

What makes this guide practical?

- Tools to help you feel less overwhelmed and have a place to look up the necessary evils of running your own business.
- Methods to address the portion of business operations that you dread but must accept because it comes part and parcel with that which energizes you.
- Processes that bring certainty of the rewards you deserve for taking the risk of starting a business.

That means this book will appeal to a broad spectrum of entrepreneurs, all who are prepared to take the risk and responsibilities that come with ownership. It would be foolish for me to think when addressing a space as big as the millions of small businesses that it is possible to segment entrepreneurs or the types of business they have easily, but I do think there are two distinct categories of readers that this book will resonate with; they are:

Independence Seekers

You plan to or are currently operating a business with the goal of being self-employed. Your focus is on a lifestyle and creative pursuit critical for you and your purpose. You are looking to fully support your lifestyle by being a Self-published Author, Designer, Freelance Editor, Contractor, or running a home-based business—you name it—but you are looking to create a low hassle lifestyle.

1. You are looking to start a business that will give you the freedom you desire, and you are looking for tools to help you build the operations right the first time. Your proactive nature has attracted you to this book to get the processes and procedures in place so that you do not experience some of the bumps in the road you have been told about.
2. Your business is growing, and you are starting to feel overwhelmed. The purpose of the business is to give you freedom and independence, not dominate your life. You need tools to help you get organized, manage your business, and to systematize your operation.

Traditional Small Business

1. You are looking to start up a business based on an idea you

have. This is a more complex operation that will likely have employees, infrastructure, and require outside funding. You want a resource guide that can help you put together your plan to get the operation off the ground and then also give you tools to bring order to the chaos of a new high-growth business.
2. You are the owner of a small business that is growing, or you look to initiate growth and need some planning and operating tools to help you make your plans a reality.

While these are two distinct audiences, there is more in common than is different. The common thread is your desire to take charge and create a new reality. If this is what you seek, this guide offers practical tools to help you get after your dreams and do so in a way that reduces the risk of failure and clarifies your vision to make it attainable.

No matter why you started your venture or if you're just planning it now, all small business owners will, at times, feel overwhelmed and face challenging choices on the next steps for the business. This guide provides tools for you to evaluate those choices and mitigate the risks of ownership.

As part of your purchase of this book, you will get free access to a secure section of http://Middle-MarketPlace.com where you will get access to all the spreadsheet and files shown in the book. This is over 6 different files at the time of this writing.

ACKNOWLEDGMENTS

Any good Journey has companions, Dorthy had the tin man, lion and scarecrow, Bilbo had the Dwarves and with this book, you won't be alone.

Your journey to build your business will be more enjoyable with companions, and there are so many in this book; you have me as your guide, and you have the countless others that I draw from either stories, interviews, or materials I have found, books I have read, experiences I have had, conversations and seminars attended. This is a compendium drawn from hundreds of sources and includes what I feel are some of the best ideas around. Anything original in the book is, in some way, inspired by others, and for that, I thank the countless people over the years that have inspired me and challenged me to write this book.

CAVEAT, DISCLAIMER, SAFE HARBOR DISCLOSURE

Please keep in mind that what you will learn from this book is advice written by a stranger who is unfamiliar with your business. Some of the topics discussed touch on Federal, State, Local taxes, and legal structures. You should always consult a professional that is familiar with your situation if you are unsure.

If you are not comfortable with your ability to discern your situation and evaluate these options on your own, then consult a lawyer and accountant now. I am passing along what I have learned from my experiences in the hope that you minimize the costs and risks that come with being self-employed.

INTRODUCTION

It happens to every business. The coming of age. A point where there needs to be a change, and if thinking or processes don't change, then the business will always be a one person show. You may have a staff but you, as the owner, are the constraining factor of the business.

The Small Business Administration publishes data that reports that half the people in the United States work for a business with less than 500 employees (the SBA definition of a Small Business) or are self-employed. The clear majority of small businesses are sole proprietors or less than five employees. Our economy is built on a foundation of millions of small businesses. This is not a new revelation; the country's economic engine has been driven for generations by proprietors of small businesses. The difference today is the ease of starting a small business and the relatively low cost to do so. If your plan is to start a business, now is an optimal time.

I have been around long enough to have experienced the benefit from the cost reduction of information technology. In the past, I paid hundreds of thousands of dollars for accounting systems, computers, and network equipment. Today, you can get an online presence and cloud-based accounting for less than a hundred dollars a month.

Our culture has also changed, and now people are used to telecommuting or working from a home office, even if you are employed by a large corporation. The table is set for anyone who wants to be their own boss to strike out on their own and have a career that is aligned with what you see as your purpose.

How is this book different from other Business guides?

Most books start with the how, what, why, and when of planning your dream. All that stuff is important and included for you, but rather than targeting an audience that right now only has a dream, I wanted to provide content that would help those of us that are looking for tools to optimize a business they have been running for some time and are looking for some ways to get personally organized.

My first approach is a focus on you as the owner. Planning your time and what you focus on has a direct correlation to the level of chaos in your business and how well the business can perform. Rather than starting with a three to five-year business plan and then figuring out how you can make this ambitious plan happen, I believe you should, instead, plan your time and align the business to your schedule and time resources.

Why?

If you are a solo operator, it is obvious the only time to draw on is yours, but for those of you with a staff and more of a leadership role, how you manage your time still drives the business and, more importantly, how you feel about your business. Without deliberately planning to work on the fun strategic stuff that got you in the business in the first place, you will burn out. I will show you how to fix that in the planning section.

Another way this book is different is by focusing on actionable advice. I am a big believer in "A bold action today on a good plan will yield better results than the perfect plan tomorrow." Considering that thinking, this book is designed to touch on many topics and provide some theory and then a practice to undertake; taking on the practices and making them a habit will build in risk reduction and productivity. Even if you're not doing exactly as designed, you will get results. I would rather you have a quick read of a section, find a solution you think will help, and try it out—this will give you the best combination of book learning and trial and error to propel your business forward.

I am also conducting an experiment with how this book will continue to provide meaningful information to you over time. Self-publishing has made it possible for those who create content to get it out to an audience and to get some income from the provision of that content. There also seems to be a trend to serialize the content sometimes to keep the message short and sweet other times to build an ongoing revenue stream for an audience to consume. My goal is to have this guide become your go-to book and the content to evergreen through collaboration.

To explain this further, let me start with a story:

One of my first classes at Chicago Booth was Financial Accounting with Roman Weil. Roman is known for his expertise in accounting, and his unique teaching style. One of his decrees was that you had two options to answer a question he asked: the first was the right answer; the second was to say "I don't know. I will look it up." After which, he would tell you the page of the book he wrote for you to recite the answer he was looking for you to give him.

It is good advice that rather than concocting some answer, just go look it up. This is my goal—to create a book that when you think, "I don't know," you reach for this book to look it up.

I acknowledge that while I have start-up, fundraising, and operations experience in a small business and have some tips to pass on, I am in no way the end-all and be-all of experts. If I want this to be the last book you should buy as a guide to starting a business and provide you a single source to go to when you don't know and need to look it up, then I need to get access to experts and content through collaboration.

Here is where Roman, again, is an inspiration. Roman offered five dollars for anyone that could find a spelling, grammatical, or accounting error in his book. As you can see below, I found one. I wish I could remember, but it earned me this check.

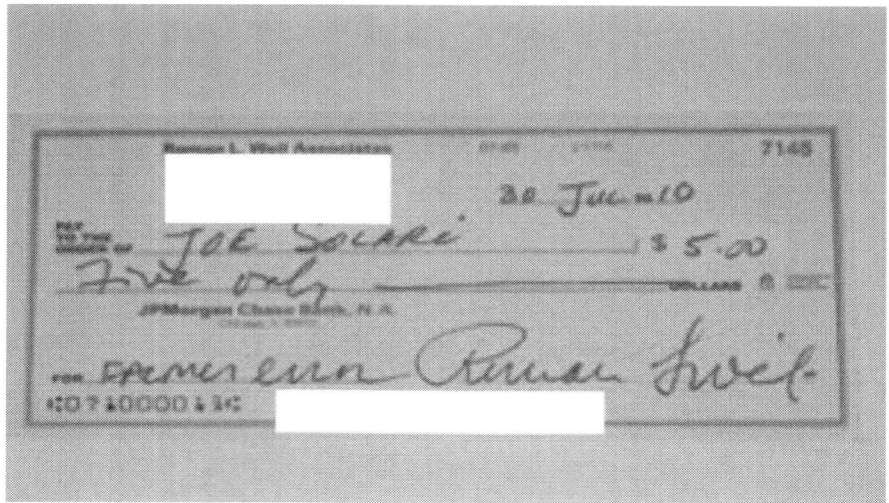

This inspired the idea that while I can put everything that I should offer in this book, you and all the other entrepreneurs have your own experiences, hacks, and tools that are just as important to get out to others who read this book. Those who are inspired by this book to take the leap into a new venture will also discover something great that can be shared with other readers. What you may wish to share is how one of the tools helped you or some new technique you developed to reduce risk.

To facilitate the feedback loop, I ask that you send me your stories of how you applied what you learned in the book to achieve your goal of starting a business or improve the business you already have. You can also write me with additions of some of your favorite tools or tricks. If I include your contribution in future versions of this book, <u>I will send you a check for five dollars</u>. I also will regularly update the e-book and have updated material available to prior purchasers of this book on the website so your initial investment will improve in value. The more we collaborate, the better this resource guide will become, and you will be assured that the content will remain evergreen.

If you have two ideas included, you end up turning a profit on this book!

Collectively, we can create a guide for the Small Business Universe, and because you purchased it, you will have access to the collective knowledge of a group of self-starters that have taken risks to create value and, more importantly, want to help others by sharing their experiences. Simply e-mail me at bizidea@middle-marketplace.com with your idea, and we can get it in the next edition. Along with your juicy $5 check, you will get credit in the book for your idea, and your name will be forever sung in the halls of Entrepreneurial Valhalla.

This is version 1.0

This is more than a book on how to start up a business; it is an experiment to tap into the collective wisdom of risk takers and then distill that wisdom to tools to reduce risk and accelerate growth while keeping you on your purpose.

I have always been creative and a risk taker. While this has not always worked out, I have not been deterred from continuing to try and create value. I believe that creativity and imagination are in the DNA, and people born with these traits will always be drawn to create, and when they are not able to do so, part of their soul will be empty.

I know that to be better at creating value and minimizing the risk, there are skills, methods, and processes that mitigate risk and amplify the ability to perform. These skills and methods can be learned just like riding a bike.

I have had some interesting experiences that I think are valuable and worth sharing. I have had the experience of bootstrapping a start-up where we grew the business within the confines of our savings and operating cash flows. I also have been through the process of raising private and institutional money and was able to raise 21.5 million dollars in eighteen months. This is a very different process and has its pros and cons. I also have been a witness (and part-time assistant) to my beautiful wife, Suze, starting her styling business and publishing e-books. Again, very different but an avenue to creating a meaningful career that aligned with her purpose.

In some respects, these experiences were different, and in others, the same, and this brings me to the second point where I believe this book is different—the focus on risk reduction. Every one of my past ventures had risks—the risks of losing money, time, or value. Anyone that has been in a startup knows how much time and money it takes to create value. No matter how committed to the dream you may be, economic downturns and poor planning can quickly turn years of work into months of crisis. Reducing the number of sleepless nights and expediting the growth of your plan to create a revenue stream is the goal of this book.

At no other time in history has it been so easy for an individual to start their own business. Where, in the past, you were required to have significant startup capital to build the infrastructure for a business, today you can get a product made, marketed, sold, and distributed with virtually no infrastructure and at a fraction of the cost. The economy has been democratized, and while this can be confusing and disruptive, it provides the tools for anyone to strike out into new frontiers.

For example, you can start a business today selling hard products such as pet costumes and never physically touch the product. You can source overseas or local product then using Fulfillment by Amazon to take delivery, store, transact, ship, and sell your product. In the past, to set up an import and distribution business required significant upfront capital a location and headcount to manage orders and pick, pack, and ship. Not today.

So, where from here?

The book has sections after we talk about risk. The sections are:

Risk & Return: The section discusses the risks associated with business ownership and how to calculate and capture the return you deserve for taking that risk. While I do discuss the headwinds of small business and attrition rate, the section is not all doom and gloom; it covers growth rate and what is the right growth rate for a business and determining the appropriate return for your business.

Ownership: This section covers the demographics of the business worked from the Fortune 500 down to the bottom of the foundation of the economy, the millions of single employee businesses that drive the economy. We discuss exit strategy along with methods for becoming an owner of a business.

Incorporation: For those of you that have a business but have not set up a State Charter, this section covers the types of entities and the tax and operational impact of each form.

Financial Command: A comprehensive section on the tools and reports for running a business. Skip the MBA and dig deep here, and you will have all the tips and tools to give you confidence in financial reporting and better yet the ability to manage the fuel of every business—CASH—so that you don't have to continually fight to get out of a cash flow cycle.

Financing Your Business: Most business plans fail to have a sound funding foundation. You can get into just as much trouble growing too fast as too slow. This section covers the types of capital and sources of funding for a start-up or growth funding and includes ideas about bootstrapping, start-up funding, venture capital, private equity, and crowdfunding.

Operations: Here, I cover a range of topics that impact the mechanics of your business. This includes Inventory, Products, Marketing, and other topics. This is not comprehensive but touches on key areas of a business I have seen need special attention.

Planning: This section provides extra tools that may have been touched on in sections one and two that are focused on what are best practices in planning your venture.

Others: There are further chapters hitting on taxes, financial modeling, ratios you should know, checklists, and other materials that tie into the main sections.

Files & Worksheets

Throughout this book, you will see reference to worksheets, checklists, or other files. By going to https://middle-marketplace.com/BOCfiles/ and signing up, you will get access to these files for your use. There is also added content that supplements some of the more complex worksheets with additional directions.

Finally, the book is laid out sequentially, but I also hope that effectiveness takes priority. If a certain section resonates with you, my hope is that you can turn to it, read the theoretical, then dig into the practical and find something you can apply immediately. I am a true believer in acting rather than contemplating the plan. So, if you have an urgent issue like cash flow or a pricing issue, go to those topics and get digging into the causes rather than reading this book front to back.

PART ONE
GETTING STARTED

BEING YOUR OWN BOSS

IN THIS SECTION, I will help you explore two central topics critical to your success as a business owner.

The first topic is Risk and Return. If you own your own business or are going to go down this path, there needs to be a reward. Yes, independence and walking to the beat of your own drum is part of it, but there needs to be a financial reward for taking the risks that come with owning a business. I will go through how I think about risk how it presents to a business. Risk management is not only avoiding bad circumstances but also planning for growth that strikes a balance between getting to your goal and having the resources to endure downturns. Learning to plan for the right growth rate and how to deliver the appropriate return for you and/or your investors is what separates successful business owners from people who happen to work at a business they own.

Next, I will go into how to become your own boss and some ways to do so. What is included is not rah-rah platitudes to how much better off you will be as a solopreneur, but an objective analysis of several paths to owning your own business and processes to do so. For many, this section will be eye opening as to options they have. If you already have your own business, you may want to skip some of that chapter as it goes into details of startups, franchises, and buying businesses.

I would suggest reading the small business demographics to get a feel for the marketplace and various size segments that make up the US economy. Knowing where your company slots in will clarify options you have for financing and other tools.

RISK & RETURN

RISK

Nobody sets out to fail, but the possibility of failure increases when you stretch yourself. Personal and financial growth happen in a zone where you will be uncertain and uncomfortable—we call this taking a risk.

It is commonly accepted in weightlifting that you will have to try to lift weights that are too heavy and fail before you finally get your strength and form to the point to where it is possible to set a new personal or world record. Using this analogy for your business, we want to limit your business fails to a missed lift, not blow out the back of your business. All business owners try to grow the business through the introduction of new products, services, or marketing and not all will be successful, so this risk section is to get a level set on your thinking about risk taking and learn some tools to limit and evaluate risk.

While it may be true that great rewards can come from taking big risks, those risks should be calculated and evaluated to fully understand the shortest path to success and what the path of failure looks like so that when you find you're going down it, you can turn around as soon as possible. Being a risk taker does not mean we should be wanton and reckless. Risk taking is about getting the risk reward ratio tilted in your favor; to do that, you need to know how to measure risk. Later in this section, we will go over return on investment—the other side of the risk-reward coin. Return on investment is a way of evaluating if the returns created by the investment were favorable in the context of the risk that you took.

Most entrepreneurs have a skewed view of risk. They do not see the risks they take in the same light as others nor do they expect to get the same returns as others. They are prepared to take far more risk with a lower return as long as they get the opportunity to try and make the dream come true. Here is the risk dichotomy of financial investors and entrepreneurs, Investors are detached from the creative process and the value it has for the founder hence they seek a financial return. You need to assure that your work and the risk you take delivers you a financial return similar to the expectations an outside investor has for the same risk.

Financial Investors have a return expectation. Their money is put to work in a business, and it comes back with a return, and by looking at this return over a fixed period, the performance of the investment can be compared to other investments. Contrast this to an owner investing time and money in their business with a willingness to differ any return until they get to their vision of what the business is to be.

Conversely, when an Entrepreneur sells a business, they typically have trouble with the valuation of the business. They value all the work they have done and the emotions and history associated with getting the business to where it is rather than the current and future cash flows the business can generate. At exit, the owner wants a premium for all the work they discounted while building the business.

To put it another way, Business owners place more weight on the freedom and autonomy they get from running a business then they do the pure financial return. If this were not the case, then the owners would have personal goals around returns similar to financial investors. We will dig deeper into these concepts in financing.

Rather than believing you are immune to failure, I suggest taking an approach where you develop risk assessing skills to analyze and plan to limit risk. Try to practice humility and honesty with what you know and don't know and design your business and practices in a way that hardens your business to adversity. The more durable your business is, the more time you will have to react and correct course when you find yourself in adverse conditions.

By the end of this book, you should have learned to react quickly and unemotionally when alerted to potential problems that could torpedo your venture. You will also learn how to quantify and deliver a return to yourself for the risks you have taken. As the owner, you will need to have a split personality and, at times, act like a gutsy risk-taking self-starter and, other times, the reserved financial investor of the business that has expectations as to the financial return that will be achieved by a risk-reward scenario you take on.

I had the distinct pleasure of hearing Richard Thaler speak in London a few years back on over confidence. Here is a link to an article Thaler wrote on the topic. My take away from his lecture was:

1. We think we are better than average at guessing.
2. We put too much weight on our guesses because of our expertise in the field.
3. We are terrible at making estimates and guesses.
4. Eventually, we are surprised by our results not falling in line with our forecasts based on our below average guessing.

Let's try an over confidence experiment while learning about the odds you face keeping the doors open on a new venture.

In the next pages, two rates related to business risk will be discussed. The first is attrition rate, i.e., the probability that your business goes out of business in each year. Then we will discuss a more positive aspect, i.e., growth rate, or what you expect your business to grow in a year. Different ends of the spectrum but both rates are important for an owner to understand.

Write down what you think the chance is for your business to fail in the current year and the age of your business. For example, "I think the rate is X% of failure and my business is two years old," or "I am starting my business, and I think the chance of failure is X%."

To be clear you must evaluating a risk, such as leaving your day job to give your venture your full attention, something where you begin fearing of failure or worry about lose of the status quo.

Later, I will show you my calculations for attrition rate for the first ten years of a business—for you to evaluate your guess against. Then we will discuss growth rates and the uncertainty associated with determining growth.

Attrition Rate

The Small Business Administration (SBA) publishes Establishment Survivability Statistics. The data comes from the SBA and US Census of small business and shows over the period of ten years the probability of an enterprise being in existence at the end of a year after its inception.

On average 750,000 businesses start up each year. According to the SBA, in the first year, 78.5% of the businesses survive year one, leaving 588,750. By year five, only 361,500 of that cohort are still doing business. What the SBA statistics don't tell us is why the business did not survive. It could be that they are bought, go out of business; there is no segmentation of positive or negative outcomes, so we don't know why they no longer exist—just that they are gone.

The charts below show that regardless of birth year or industry, the results are similar. The business you run or the one you will start will be no different. If you act as if it is, you are being overconfident.

Chart 1: Shows that regardless of vintage, the attrition curve is highly correlated. When you started, your business does not influence the curve of the first five years or significant deviation because of any circumstances. For example, the great recession the bankruptcy rate increased from 2008 through 2010, resulting in over one million bankruptcies, but we don't see this as a spike in any specific vintage. We can surmise it hits all the same. The time frame would be year three on the blue line and year eight on the green line, but in both cases, there is no noticeable difference.

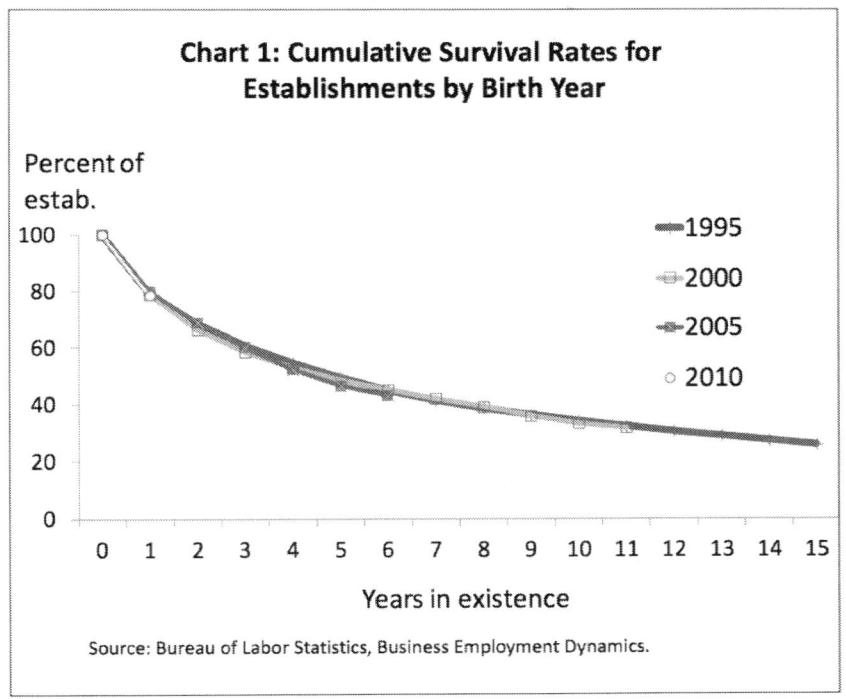

Chart two shows different industries and attrition over time. There is some variation in the noted industries but all track a similar decline over time, giving credence that there is no industry that does not share the characteristic that time is a significant enemy.

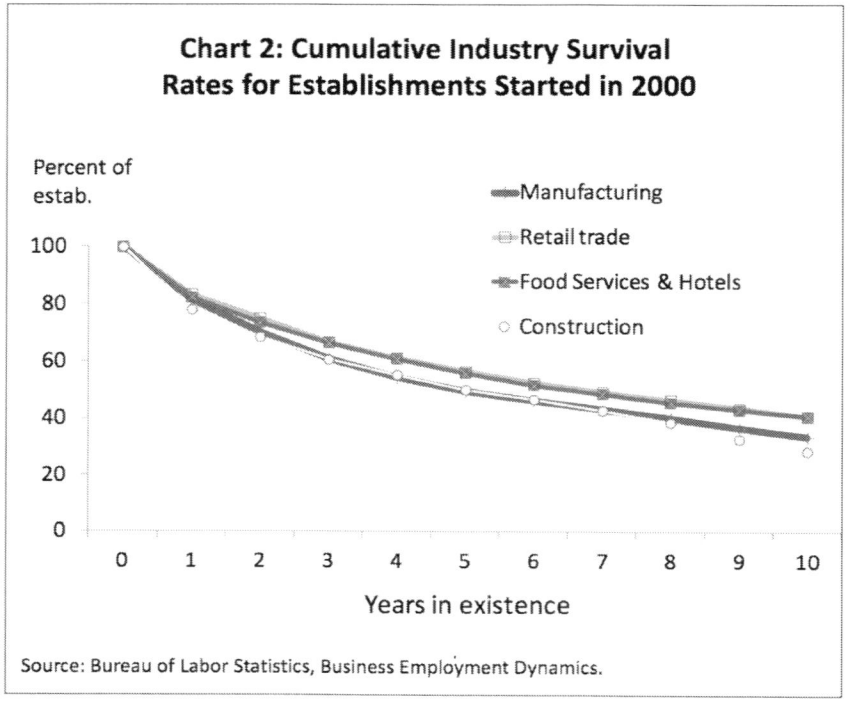

The above data is used by the SBA to determine average survival rates by years since startup—this chart is below. The data is based on scores of cohorts over decades with average startups each year between 500,000 to an 800,000 a year with little variation in the results.

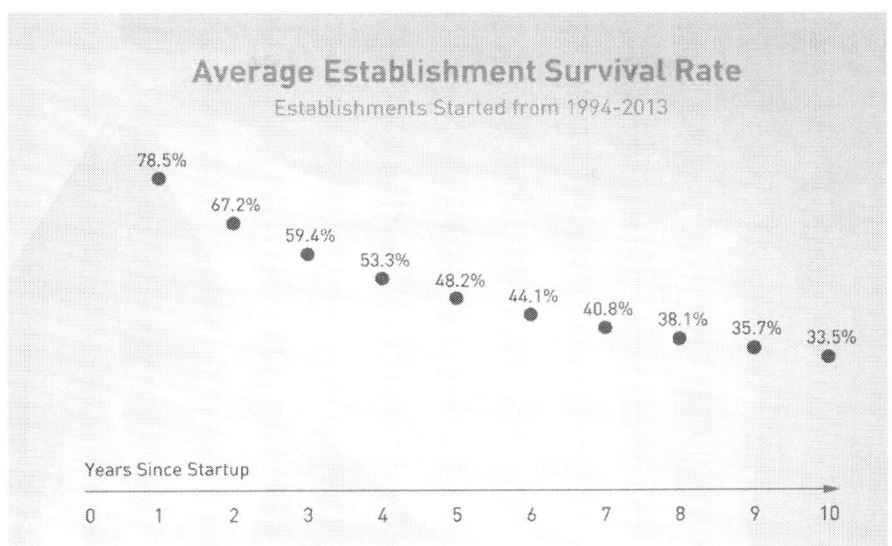

The attrition rates of the first ten years are listed in the table below. Over time, the attrition rate drops considerably each year for the first few years, and by year seven, the attrition rate is one-third of what it was in year one.

Sample	750,000									
Year	1	2	3	4	5	6	7	8	9	10
Attrition	21.5%	14.4%	11.6%	10.3%	9.6%	8.5%	7.5%	6.6%	6.3%	6.2%
Survival Rate	78.5%	67.2%	59.4%	53.3%	48.2%	44.1%	40.8%	38.1%	35.7%	33.5%
Survivors	588,750	504,000	445,500	399,750	361,500	330,750	306,000	285,750	267,750	251,250

The attrition rate should be viewed as your probability of going out of business in each year. The data shows that regardless of the year you start or the business you choose, the odds are the same, and special care needs to be taken in evaluating your risks in the first forty-eight months of operation.

If your business is older than ten years, then it is around 6% attrition.

How did your guess on the probability of failure compare to the table above?

Do you accept that your business is no different than any other of a similar vintage and therefore has a 6–21.5% probability of failure?

How are you planning to mitigate this risk?

None of the above is meant to scare you away from your dream of starting your own business. Rather, it is to help you to harden your business to adversity. To plan for what could happen.

People that survive accidents, fires and assaults do so because they have imagined themselves in these situations and developed a plan for how to act. You have a higher probability of surviving a home fire if you have thought through all the escape routes from home. Then when the actual event happens, and adrenalin is flowing, and shock is setting in, your reaction will be to act as you had imagined rather than be stuck trying to figure out a complex solution in a state of fear.

Business emergencies are no different. By accepting that your business, while special to you, is one in 750,000 that started the year you formed your business and that it has the same probabilities (33%) of being in business in a decade, you have a higher chance of beating the odds. Understanding that the first forty-eight months of a business present the highest attrition period may be what gets you through that red zone. But it won't be because you can spout off the facts; it will be because your acceptance of those facts influences you to plan better and be more vigilant of the warning signs. It's not that you know the information; it is what you do with that information that will make the difference. I would argue that if you are reading this and make the conscious decision to apply the planning and monitoring tools I have collected, you have a higher probability of surviving an event that would close the doors another business.

Growth Rate

What does growth rate have to do with risk? The basis of your business's success is that it will grow and sustain a level of sales that will support your plan. Without this growth, the time and capital you plan to put at risk will be lost. This begs the next question to test your ability to evaluate and predict the future.

What growth rate should you use for the next five years for your business if you were to write a plan?

Pick an annual growth rate and write it down.

When I have asked business owners what was the situation that caused the business to fail or get close to failure, they site unforeseen circumstance, most notably the overall economy. They may have been in an industry that was motoring along and then the economy or industry took a turn. It could be the housing and credit crisis or the recent downturn in oil price, but when it changed, it really changed and changed fast!

A business plan that you are developing could have the assumption that your business will grow at an average of GPD, say 3.5% per year. GDP is the most common proxy for growth projections. You might also use GDP as a base for growth and stipulate in your plan that because of your product or sale process that you expect sales to grow at two times GDP or five percent above GDP. Many business plans are based on linear growth tied to GDP, sometimes with a low, base, and optimistic case to provide investors with more than a single growth projection to reference.

Remember the earlier question? Did you pick a growth rate associated with GDP, maybe even 3.5% exactly? Well, here is the problem.

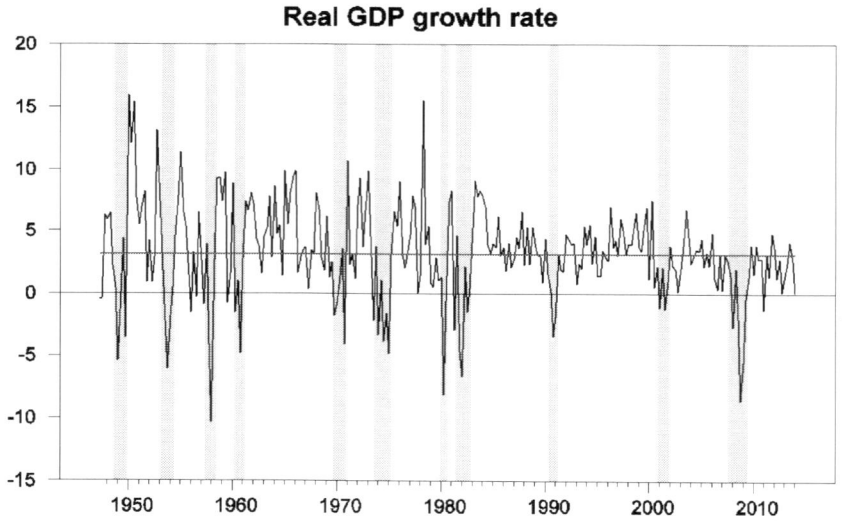

The chart above shows the Gross Domestic Product (GDP) growth rate from 1945 through 2014. Notice how the average is 3.5% but notice how widely the numbers from year to year swing.

To have 95% confidence in your assumption for next year's growth, you need to apply the standard deviation of 6.5% to the average of 3.5% to derive a 95% confidence interval of -9.5% to 16.5%.

To complicate matters, that is only for one year; the next year is independent of the prior year. So, as we can see from the chart above, you can have a year that has 5% growth followed by -9%.

Later in the book, I will cover how to use some techniques to create business models with this type of variation and then show you how to use it to calculate probabilities of success and failure. The main takeaway is that if you are not being respectful of the force of the economy and what it does to a business when it whipsaws through an economic shock, you are, again, being overconfident.

Therefore, underlying any growth trajectories you have for your business, you may need to pay attention to macroeconomic trends and associate the two. For example, rather than saying "My business will grow at 5% a year," you look at past performance against an indicator like GDP and learn that you grow at 3.5% above GDP or double GDP.

Validating your growth rate and associating it to the larger economy helps you in two ways:

1. You now can develop better projections when planning.

2. If you look to raise money or increase sales, being able to confidently demonstrate your business growth rate and how it is associated with the economy becomes an "element of value" in your business that a buyer or investor will pay a premium for over other businesses.

Return on Investment

Why are you taking Risk? For the reward, the expectation is that your hard work and capital invested will result in the creation of value beyond what was put in—a return on investment. For every dollar of effort or real capital, you are planning on it creating more.

We want to build a hardened adversity resistant machine that takes your inputs of creativity, sweat, and capital and converts them into the outputs cash, and giving you and those involved in your venture Joy and fulfillment of purpose.

Return on Creativity

If your venture is built on your creativity, we need to have this venture convert your ideas into cash. The real magic of your creativity is that this is a wellspring that you can continue to tap into. Your creativity is something your competitors cannot reproduce and provides a true competitive advantage. If you create a process that turns your creativity into a product that others can use, then you can keep producing and providing others with your content. The problem that most creatives face is that they become overwhelmed or don't even know where to start when it comes to building and maintaining the machine that can produce and scale system to produce a return on investment.

The difference between successful independent authors and those that can't develop a growing income from writing is the struggle around the work needed to market books and develop a business system that connects with the target audience. They may not have the tools to develop the business and maintain the financial engine and see these "business stuff" as a distraction from their joy and purpose of writing. To get a continuing return on your creativity, some work will need to go towards systemizing the marketing and sales of the creative product.

Now you may not be very creative; that is OK. While you won't have the creativity to leverage, you can still apply effort into the other two areas to fuel your ROI Machine.

Return on Sweat

As the owner, your hard work will be the biggest driver of the machine. We do need to make sure that the machine is designed in such a way that the work that you do delivers a financial return and personal fulfillment. All too often, the owner loses sight of why they started the business in the first place, and they no longer get energy from the business through feeling fulfilled.

Along with fulfillment, there needs to be a return mechanism where your contribution comes back to you in a reasonable timeframe as cash. Initially, this may be a living wage that grows over time to give you the lifestyle you would like; later there will need to be work put into making sure that you can exit your business and capture the value you created.

Return on Capital Invested

Every dollar that you put in the business needs to produce more dollars. As you will see in the working capital section, as a business grows, there is cash that needs to stay in the business to keep the engine lubricated; the bigger the engine, the more the lubrication. What we need to make sure is that your business process is designed to deliberately and routinely return cash. In most cases, you will be the single biggest shareholder, and you need to make sure that your cash is getting at least the returns you could get by putting it in an index fund.

Cold Hard Cash

This is our single biggest indicator of performance. Is your venture providing you with a return? The return can come in a variety of ways.

First, it may come as a little extra money to pay some bills or take a vacation. Eventually, you work up to drawing a salary. Then you look to the business to fund benefits like retirement, education, healthcare, and other fringe benefits. Finally, there is the capital gains of distributions or funds from the sale of the business.

You should also cast a critical eye to how your capital invested comes back to you:

1. Your capital needs to start coming back at some point, and when it does, it should have a return. Keep in mind money coming back to you as a fringe benefit expensed to the business, payroll, and returned capital will all have different tax rates, and the tax impact should be part of your consideration in how you take money out of the business.

2. The capital that remains in the business needs to be growing in value. If you are doing your job right, the money you leave in the business should be your best investment opportunity. Its growth rate should be better than a like investment in the stock market.

The S&P 500 from 1928 through the end of 2015 resulted in a compound annual growth rate of 7.4% (that included dividends and adjusting for inflation). So, this is a benchmark. Your enterprise needs to give you at least this return on your capital invested. It is likely that you will do better than this, but we need to set a benchmark. When planning, look to this as your minimum investment goal. With that being said, if you put $1,000 in to start a business and work at it and find in two years' time it provides you a salary of $25,000, your internal rate of return is 400% and growing if you get the same or higher salary the next year. So, while there was no return of capital per se on the $1,000, you are already generating a healthy return and knowing how to identify this and quantify it will give you a great sense of accomplishment and help you to communicate to others your business results.

Joy and Purpose fulfillment

People are motivated to start their own business because they look to find the appropriate outlet for their creativity or drive. When this happens, and your daily actions align with your purpose, you gain new energy and a source of joy. If you get this alignment, you will be joyful —even when you may be in unfortunate circumstances. You can still tap into your joy and push through, as you know that this, too, shall pass. While this may be hard to quantify, we need to make sure that your venture provides the added value of making you want to jump out of bed to get your day started.

As a business gets more complex, you may find that there are parts of the business that overwhelm you, steal your joy, or you just can't comprehend. It is these parts that will need to be modified to minimize the interaction and to provide you with a process that delivers the best results with the least amount of effort. We will discuss this in detail in the planning section.

Capital Preservation

Preservation of capital is a critical concept of risk reduction and return generation. The only thing that drives an Investor more than greed for a return on capital is fear of that capital being sent to Heaven. The primary capital to preserve is your own. Too many owners forget to treat their time like money and their money like an outside investor would. Changing this mindset will not only help you to better evaluate risk and reward but also help you to gain a deeper understanding of your accomplishments while growing the business. It can be hard when running a solo lean organization to quantify the progress you are making.

If you decide to seek investors, they will put a premium on their capital over your sweat and vision. More importantly, you should treat your time and money like an investor. You need to have a split personality and look at your decisions as both a visionary creator and risk taker and as an Investor and risk mitigator. Why? Because you ARE both.

We will go in depth on how applying financial disciple helps you to be a better operator and build your ROI machine. Even if you are not a numbers person, there are suggestions that strike a balance between bean counting and sticking your head in the sand that are easy to adopt and help to reduce risk and eliminate your feelings of frustration and being overwhelmed.

You decide what you need from a variety of tools that you can pick and choose from based on the complexity that your venture has and the need for structure. The more you adopt and systematize, the more reliable returns will be for your business.

Return on Investment ROI

Every project or growth initiative you undertake you should look at from the perspective of return on investment. If the Machine is built right, the obvious choice for where your money should be is invested in your business. Working to make sure that every dollar that sits in your machine as working capital produces a dollar plus at least 7.4 % achieves this. Our goal is to double the return of the S&P 500 making your dream job a wealth creation system that is also tied to your purpose and creativity. To achieve this, we will look to get an ROI between 6.8 and 13.6% for your business as it grows. What we need to keep in mind is that you're going to be investing cash, creativity, and sweat into the business and we need to figure out the return over time.

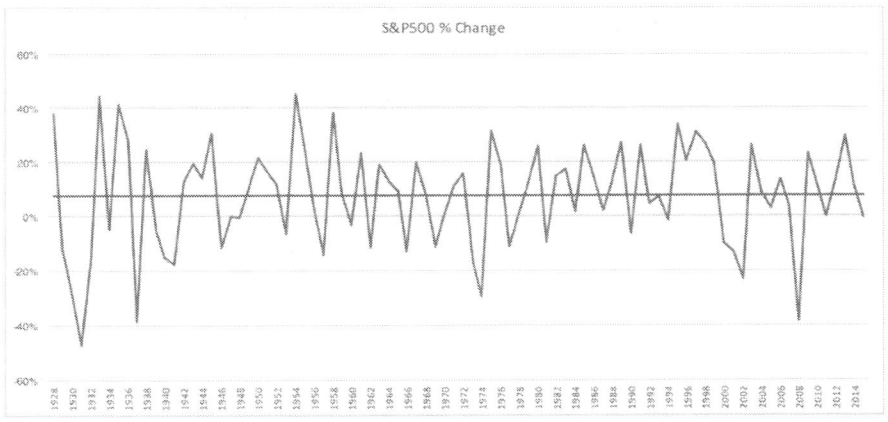

The book goes into detail about a range of ratios to know in the operations section, but at this point, it is important to get an understanding of the different types of returns measurement and what they mean.

An annual return of 6.8% means that if you put $100 in an investment, at the end of the year, you would have 106.80; at the end of year two, it would be 114.06 ($100+ $6.80 for year one; $106.80 + $7.26 for year two). In this case, the annual rate of return is the same in both years, so it is also the internal rate of return. Internal Rate of Return is a formula used in finance that determines the rate of return on an investment over a period of time or when the cash flows from the investment vary.

Here are some examples as to how IRR works and ways to think about it for your business. The great thing is, you don't need to worry about the formula because it can be easily calculated in excel and numbers with the IRR function. I have provided the formula embedded into the IRR worksheet for you to use.

	Year 1	Year 2	Year 3	IRR
Example 1	-$1,000	$0	$25,000	400%
Example 2				
Cash	-$1,000		$25,000	
Sweat	-$5,000	-$5,000	-$5,000	
Total	-$6,000	-$5,000	$20,000	46%
Example 3				
Cash	-$1,000		$18,410	
Sweat	-$5,000	-$5,000	-$5,000	
Total	-$6,000	-$5,000	$13,410	13.5%

Example 1: You start a business making and selling some product. You initially invest $1,000 in cash to get the business started. You then work in the business for free, and after two years of nothing, the business generates $25,000 in profit; you would calculate the return to be 400%. WOW!

Example 2: Same scenario, but we also count your sweat labor as a cost of $5,000 a year for all three years and, again, the 20,000 in profit. This results in a 46% IRR—again terrific.

In example three, I, instead, took our scenario of a $1,000 cash investment and three years of $5,000 sweat equity and then determined the amount of profit needed to hit our top goal of 13.6%. The result was $13,410 in profit; to hit the 6.8% hurdle would require $12,184 in profit.

If you can create a small-scale operation that generates a return between

6–12%, then the logical place for you (and others) to invest is in that business.

If you create a return on investment machine that cranks out the types of returns we discussed, then you have a business that money needs, not a business that needs money. While you may still require working capital to scale, you won't have trouble getting that capital because you can show potential investors where the business had been doing with your money. The problem most investors face is, they are being asked to provide venture capital rather than growth capital; the difference being that the business model and returns have not been proven out and the risks are much higher.

You can download the IRR worksheet from https://middle-marketplace.com/BOCfiles/

The IRR Worksheet shows some simple IRR calculations and Net Present value calculations for you to evaluate performance and investment in your business. These tools are useful for the evaluation of expenditure of capital for assets or growth initiatives.

Risk Summarized

Here is the most important reason to understand the risks you plan to undertake. You are setting out on this new journey that will impact your whole life, how you plan to earn a living, what you will do for the rest of your life, as well as impact the lives of your family, employees, and investors. It is a lot of responsibility. You are going to lose a lot of sleep.

The business of the future that you envision today will be built by your effort, and you will likely be the largest investor or one of the largest;

therefore, you have the most time and money at risk. Taking the time to quantify the risks you face and do some planning will benefit you and your loved ones the most.

Here are some points to keep in mind as you think about quantifying and planning for your business:

1. The first way to mitigate risk is to understand and quantify that risk.

2. Estimating the probability of something happening helps you to get emotion out of your decision-making process and look at the future outcomes with some objectivity.

3. You need to harden your business to adversity and uncertainty.

4. You need the tools in place to alert you to changes stressing your business.

5. When the day comes that could put you "out of business," you have the ability and time to adapt to what comes your way and make the most of it, if you have considered and planned for the adversity. Your goal should be that when the unfortunate and unexpected occurs, you go to the tools you have learned to turn the lemons into lemonade.

6. Risk is real; acceptance and planning for some adversity is prudent.

Summarizing Risk

Those who start new ventures or seek business ownership have higher risk tolerance. You tend to minimize risk, and those who start new ventures, in my experience, are past that tipping point of having risk be a hurdle to the new venture. Optimism and tenacity are your mental remedy to concerns about future risk and uncertainty. The risk adverse tend to never expose themselves to situations where they will be at risk, so they are far less likely to be business owners. For those of us that find ourselves running a business, we should push ourselves to frame the risks we take and evaluate the impact that will have on the business. We suffer from an overconfidence bias; it is a pathological disease. We just need to make sure it becomes terminal. Our remedy needs to be risk vigilance, and using tools to visualize the risks we take gets payoffs near short and long term for these risks and harden the business to risk taking.

BUSINESS DEMOGRAPHICS

WHAT IS A SMALL BUSINESS?

Small business is a vague term, and for you to best understand how your business fits in the context of all other businesses, it is good to have a solid understanding of the sizes and characteristics of all the businesses in the country. The problem is getting good information and then putting into the frame of reference. This section has a collection of research that I believe presents the best picture of the number of businesses and their size.

It is important to get clarity on the different business sizes and characteristics as you go through this book. The size of a business impacts the following:

- The value of the business
- Who is a potential buyer?
- How you should think about selling the business
- What type of financing is available?

For example, when discussing ownership through acquisition, the type of business that you might be thinking about buying and how a deal could be structured will be heavily influenced by the company size.

In doing research for this book, I spent time digging into what demographic are for US businesses. The SBA cites 28 million businesses in the United States and most of these being small businesses (99.9%). The SBA definition is very broad, being:

"an independent business with fewer than five hundred employees."

The SBA number is all over the internet and used in articles and blogs everywhere. The problem is, there are some nuances to what they are quantifying as a business. In 2014, there the US Census (the actual source of the data the SBA cites) identified 23,836,937 total non-employer establishments.

A nonemployer business is one that has no paid employees, has annual business receipts of $1,000 or more ($1 or more in the construction industries), and is subject to federal income taxes. Non-employer businesses are generally small, such as real estate agents and independent contractors. Non-employers constitute nearly three-quarters of all businesses, but they contribute less than four percent of overall sales and receipts data. Nonemployers are not included in the counts of establishments from the Economic Census or County Business Patterns. While these constitute businesses in the SBA number, they are corporate entities for specific projects or a single, self-employed person.

The US Census (the body responsible for collecting this type of data) and the source used by the SBA, account for 7,488,353 establishments that have employees; therefore, there is a portion of the 16,348,584 businesses that falls into what would be the traditional owner-operator type business and provides revenues that can support an individual or family but have no employees.

The second piece of data, and this is from the SBA, which leads me to believe that the number of actual businesses is lower than 28 million is that, on average, there are annually 401,000 business closures and 406,000 startups for a net increase of 5,000 new businesses. This lines up with our discussions in the section on risk the <u>attrition rate</u> is steady. Therefore, the math does not add up to build up to 28 million companies when you only create 5,000 a year; it would take over five thousand years. So many of these businesses are shells that do not serve the economy in a meaningful way.

The amount of the 28 million companies in the United States that are operating businesses supporting an individual or family is difficult to ascertain seeing as many of the establishments noted in the 28 million are tax reporting or pass through entities with little economic value. If we could determine the quantity of single operator businesses to add to approximately 7.4 million, those numbers would be heavily weighted to the micro and small business category, not evenly disturbed across, since we know these businesses do not have employees.

How would we go about figuring out more about the number of these companies, the number of employees they might have, and the revenues they generate?

Let's start out with some easy stuff to figure out the number of businesses.

The Fortune 500 constitutes the top 500 companies by sales revenue. This covers sales from 458 billion (Walmart) down through 5.1 Billion. If you look at the Fortune 1000, the smallest company on the list has 1.8 billion in sales. We know that the top 1,000 companies cover 1.8 billion in sales and up, and they don't have anything to do with small business other than as the anchor at the other end of the spectrum.

Another term that is used arbitrarily is the term Middle Market and the middle market stop and start. The National Center for the Middle Market states that the Middle Market are businesses with revenues between 10 million and 1 billion and constitute nearly 200,000 businesses.

To further delineate the number of companies, I looked at two surveys of small business—the Kaufman Foundation and the National Small Business Association. While the Kaufmann study has a larger population of companies surveyed, it doesn't segment revenues as finely as the NSBA study. Taking the revenue segmentation and applying it to the 7.4 million businesses, the following table is constructed. Where some issue of clarity is around the conflict of the arbitrary low cut-off of 10 million on the low side of the Middle Market, and the revenue categorization of five to twenty-five makes it difficult to provide company counts for five to ten million and ten to twenty-five million.

REVENUE	%	QTY	CATEGORY
0-100k	29%	3,593,659	MICRO
100-250	14%	1,734,870	MICRO
250-500	11%	1,363,112	MICRO
500-1mm	9%	1,115,274	SB
1-5MM	22%	2,726,224	SB
5-25mm	8%	991,354	SB
25-75mm	1%	123,919	LMM
75-150	0.50%	61,960	MM
150mm+	2%	247,839	MM
Fortune 1000	0.01%	1,000	FORTUNE 1000

Given the segments from that we have from the survey, we can define some market segments—the first being the micro market going through the fortune 500 businesses. What we do not know is how much we should add to the first two categories of businesses, but those categories will increase.

Micro market: $0-500,000 in Sales 4 million businesses

Small Business: $0.5-5 Million in sales 2.2 million businesses

Small to Lower Middle Market Bridge: $5-25 million 598,988 businesses

Middle Market: $25-75 million 74,874 businesses,

$75-150 million 37,442 businesses

>$150 million 149,767 businesses

Using the survey results from the Kaufmann Foundations survey in 2011, we see the propensity for businesses to have no employees (owner only) or one employee.

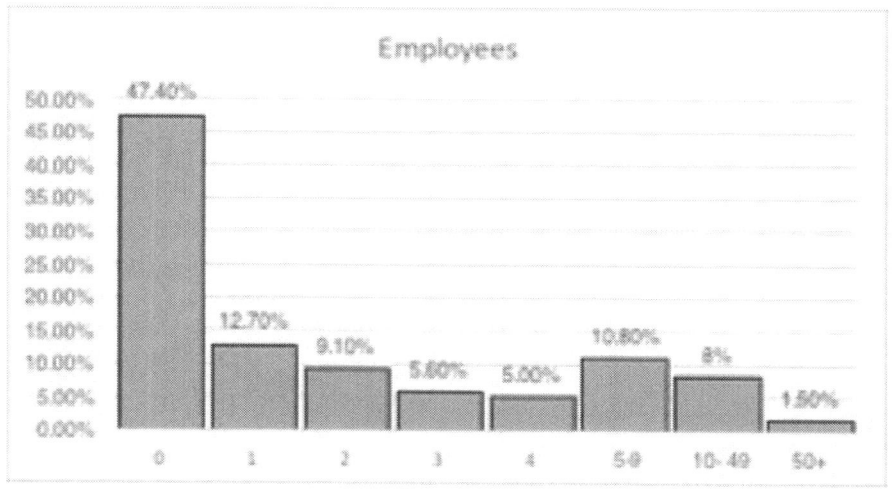

- 85% of US businesses are below five million dollars a year in sales; this is approximately 6.3 million businesses.
- 50% of businesses being below five hundred thousand in sales.
- 60% of US businesses have none or one employee.

Now you have a context for business sizes and how your startup or business compares to others.

For those of you that already have a business that is incorporated and are looking to find solutions for you and your organization, I suggest you skip ahead to Financial Command.

If you have a business but no legal entity set up, then go to "Should I Incorporate?"

OWNERSHIP

FOR THOSE CONTEMPLATING OWNING A BUSINESS, *start here.*

Most business owners don't have a deliberate plan to become an owner of a business. It is thrust upon them, usually out of circumstances related to a change in employment or economic downturn. While recessions are difficult for existing businesses and result in the demise of many firms, that same turmoil also produces new businesses. For many, the obvious solution for what's next after a job loss is to never work for someone else again and become your own boss.

I didn't seriously consider consulting and writing until I found myself out of work after the oil and gas start-up I was operating became a victim of low oil prices. Being in this situation can be quite stressful, as you weigh your opportunities and paths forward against the runway you have before your savings is gone.

The first step on your journey towards being the successful owner of a business that is aligned with your purpose and passion is to set a plan. Read through this chapter with the intent to later develop a written exit plan using the template provided in the book. For the best results, I suggest that you work through the whole book to get familiar with terms and processes and then apply this newly gained knowledge to the plan for better results. I know, in the introduction, I stated that the book is designed to be used as a piecemeal to attack specific issues in a business—and that is true if you own an existing business. But if you are just starting with an idea and figuring out your path to ownership, I suggest taking the time to go through the whole book to inform your decision-making process and planning. I guarantee it will be helpful, and this section alone may open your eyes to alternative ownership paths you were not aware were open to you.

The clarity of your plan also will improve if you begin to integrate concepts from <u>financial command</u> and <u>financing your business</u>.

Wondering where to begin to firm up your conviction and plan to become your own boss? Let's begin by analyzing where you are now and determine the best pathway to ownership for you.

What is your Current situation?

Are you currently employed or do you find yourself currently out of work and considering ownership as an option to finding another job?

Your startup can begin while you currently have a day job with the goal of you eventually becoming self-employed, or it may be something you are thrust into because of a change in circumstances. Many of us find that what first appears to be adversity is really a gift that frees us from the illusion of certainty and comfort that a wage brings.

If you are still working, then you should be planning to have your next full-time position to be as the owner of your business at a date that you have planned for. If before that date you find you voluntarily or involuntarily need to leave your current role, you have a plan and can quickly assess what you may need to adjust for your plan to be successful. A big part of this is determining the money you need to transition to self-employment; this will influence the time you need to dedicate to getting to your quitting day and thus the determination of a fixed and firm date to hit the eject button.

Savings

Later, we will explore the concept of capital, its purpose in the business, and the impact of undercapitalization. Capital is the cash and assets used to start the business and to fund its operation. It is very likely that some or all the initial capital to start your business will come from you.

You will need some startup capital to buy inventory, supplies or hire vendors. The amount of savings needed for operation of the business needs to be determined, and it is best to read through the cash flow and working capital sections to learn how to determine capital needs. In fact, if you begin by applying the business planning tools for an operating business in this early planning stage, you will have excellent estimates of how your business will work.

If you find that buying a business is interesting to you, then you must begin to save up capital to purchase the business. While you will learn later in the book about ways to finance a business, including ways to purchase a business with the help of others, your success at raising funds will be greatly improved if you also invest alongside other investors so that you have "skin in the game."

You also need to begin to estimate the funds you need to support yourself if you feel exiting your current role prior to your new business being able to support you is important for success. The same information will help if you find yourself in the situation out of work and still starting up. Many a new business has failed because the owner underestimated the time it would take to get cash flow positive, and if you're not sure what that means, then read on; you will be the end of the book.

If you are still employed, try this thought exercise. If you have just found out you will be out of work, then this isn't a thought exercise; you need to figure out how much time you must get things to ramp up. Write down the answers to these questions:

What does it cost to operate my household for one month?

What would I cut out to reduce that monthly cost?

If you are already generating side income for the idea that is the basis of your business, how much free cash flow does it generate?

How many hours are you currently spending to generate that income?

Is there a linear relationship of time and money invested to the output for the side business?

The answers to these questions will help you to quantify the cash you need to get your operation going and pay bills as you ramp up your operation.

Get your plan together for moving from the dream of ownership to the reality.

Remember back in Grade School how, at the beginning of the year, there would be practice fire drills?

The purpose of the drill is to familiarize you with what to do in case of emergency. Research shows that people have a higher survival rate if they have imagined or practiced what to do in various emergencies. Think of your exit strategy the same way. You are going to plan the exit strategy from your current position as a business owner. The intention is to have this happen at the time and place of your choosing, but if circumstances change (like they close the plant you work at), you will have to use this same plan with some adjustments to get you to that same successful exit (albeit sooner).

The topic of planning your exiting and moving from what you are doing now and beginning anew is top of mind for you; therefore, we need to broach the topic of you planning your exit from your current situation to your new life running your own business. After reading this section, you could begin to create your exit strategy. I suggest you don't until reading through the whole book—to become familiar with concepts and build a good general knowledge of how to plan your time, operate a business, and evaluate the funding you may need.

Your success begins with a plan

You could walk into your boss tomorrow and tell him you're quitting to start your own business. That's a pretty simple plan but not well thought out. You want a well thought out simple plan that will, in turn, guide you to a successful outcome. In the appendix, there is a one-page exit plan worksheet to help you think through what you need in place to exit your day job, or if you find yourself out of a job, what your runway looks like for you to get your startup and going.

This can also be used if you decide that buying a business is the choice for you. Acquisition tends to require more time and planning around getting savings pulled together that you would use to buy a business.

The plan needs to answer some questions for you. You want to be fully focused on making your new enterprise a success, not being anxious about what to do next; having this document is a great anchor for when you get anxious or uncertain to get your focus back on what matters.

The essence of the exit strategy is this:

1. A set launch date where you will leave your day job and/or the conditions of the startup that trigger leaving.

2. The conditions that need to be in place for you to begin ramping up the new business and eventually leave your day job.

3. Firm understanding of the time and money needed for your new enterprise as well as any gaps in income between leaving your day job and your new enterprise generating the income you desire.

Here are the questions you need to begin to answer in your plan to start your new business. This is not a full business plan but a way to assess what it really means to be self-employed. You may find that to make a good plan that you're confident in, you will need to supplement it with actual business planning and financial modeling.

Your Economics

Getting an understanding of your monthly personal requirements to pay your bills and get your business up and running requires first an understanding of what you're incoming, and outgoing cash is and what you will need to keep in reserve to fund the business.

Current Income

What is the current income from the job you plan to leave?

What is the current income from what you plan to base your business on? Most businesses born from moonlighting and based on a service or product you provide are already generating income or can produce income quickly given you put more effort into the operation.

Current outflow

What are your monthly cash needs to pay your bills?

When evaluating these needs, look to what your plans tell you as far as time commitment needs to get the business to grow. You will likely learn that your free time and ability to spend will be reduced to give you the capital and time you need to get things up and running.

What are you Passionate about?

Do you dream of doing something you are not doing now or do like what you're doing but would like to do it on your own terms?

If you need help figuring out what might be a good business idea, there are many books specifically focused on this subject like "Will it Fly" and "Business Model Generation" that can help you to ideate and formalize your business. If you're passionate about what you plan to do, then your ability to succeed will increase through the shear force created by your energy and enthusiasm to do the work.

Having experience in the industry even as an employee gives you experience to the ins and outs of the industry that will be beneficial to your success. If your passion is in another area, follow the passion. If you're not excited and enthused to be doing this new venture, people will smell your lack of commitment and likewise not commit to supporting you.

PATHS TO OWNERSHIP

To help you evaluate your options, here are some different pathways to business ownership. There are likely more than you may be considering. For instance, if you are currently employed at a small privately held business like the ones we have described in the demographics section and the owner is getting older, you may have a very good option to become and owner through acquisition. Prior to reading this, you or the owner may never have had this thought cross your mind, or maybe you have but struggle with how to go about buying a business. Let's begin with some options around purchasing a business rather than what most books cover in starting from scratch.

BUYING AN EXISTING BUSINESS VERSUS STARTING SOMETHING NEW

or

Buy Versus Build

I am currently working with a client that is a real estate agent. She has been contacted by the owner of the first brokerage she worked at. He is older and looking to retire and thought of my client as the type of person he thought could take over the Brokerage. (A great lesson in not burning bridges.)

This is a great example of a deal that can be a win-win if structured correctly. I believe that there are dozens of these types of deals in the market, and if you're so inclined, you can work to find and close a deal like this in an industry you're interested in if you are prepared to do the legwork.

Let's face it; not everyone is cut out to create a new business from scratch. You can have the desire and drive to be an owner, but not an interest in starting something new. You may also be good at something at the place you work and would love to continue to do this while also having the benefits of business ownership. If this describes you, there are existing opportunities to becoming the owner of a business by buying a business.

Why would buying a business be appealing?

1. An established business has made it through the risky starting years and therefore does not come with the startup failure risk.

2. If this is a business you are currently an employee at, you know the business and have experience in how it serves its clients.

3. The business has established customers, products, and services; therefore, you don't have to prove the business concept.

4. Business owners looking for options for retirement that are not big enough to attract the attention of strategic or financial buyers lack options. There are many acquisition options within twenty miles of where you live that are under everyone's radar.

5. Established businesses have better access to capital and likely have relationships with banks and creditors that can continue after the seller leaves.

Where most people begin to struggle is figuring out the process of buying a business. In the ownership through acquisition section, we will discuss how to find a business to buy, then ways to structure a deal.

In putting this section on buying a business, I imagined readers falling into two camps. The first and larger group use this information to help them to explore and buy a business they either work for or a small local business that they find through friends and family. The other group is smaller, and they take on an approach of a fundless sponsor or search fund.

Buying a business as a method for becoming an owner may be easier than you expect; there are estimates of anywhere from 700,000 to ten million businesses that are currently privately held by Baby Boomers that are reaching retirement age. While many will continue to work well past retirement age, the three D's (Disease, Divorce & Death) expedite a lot of sales. As Boomers retire, this will cause the largest generational shift of wealth in history, and given these circumstances, buying a business from an existing owner may be an option for you. One important benefit is that the business is already in operation and does not have typical issues that start-ups present.

The market for buying and selling businesses is huge and diverse and how one might go about buying a business is quite different based on the type of business you are looking to buy.

To help you understand the differences, we need to reflect on what was learned in the business demographics section, and we segmented businesses.

Buying a Job

The first category I would like to discuss is what I call buying a job. You would be purchasing a small business that provides a living for the owner/operator. The profits from the business provide the owner with a wage and some additional profits. This is a very attractive solution for becoming your own boss, as you forgo the start-up phase and take over an established business with customers and revenues. This is particularly interesting if you possess the skill set needed for the underlying business. If you have worked in HVAC repair, buying an HVAC business can be a great fit, especially if the case is: it is a business you currently work for. There are countless opportunities to buy a job in the service industry but you will need the skill set to be able to fulfill the service your self.

Buying a Business

This covers larger firms where there may be more employees and more complex business. As you look towards larger businesses that produce more profits, the number of potential buyers increases significantly. Once a business is making over $500,000 in earnings, it will attract strategic buyers (competitors) and financial buyers (Private Equity) that will be difficult to compete with.

You can play to your strengths in small and micro businesses where the number of interested parties is low and getting a deal done can be viewed as difficult or expensive versus the size of the company.

Executing deals in the smallest businesses can pose difficulties for a wide range of reasons. Primarily, it is because the seller and buyer are not experienced deal makers, and these deals are so small that business brokers don't give them much time and attention. When they do, the broker charges a significant fee that could scuttle the deal because of how much of the profit it takes out of the transaction.

Characteristics of owner/operator business deals:

- Typically, a "for sale by owner" deal, or

owners are not actively selling because they don't know where to start

- Typically purchased by an individual
- Typically purchased by someone less than twenty miles away
- Deals are difficult to finance
- Deals are difficult to find
- Deals are difficult to value

Looking at businesses that have revenues between $250,000 and one million dollars, there are, by my estimate, at least 1.49 million businesses that are operating and that potentially could be for sale. While we can't determine the actual amount from the data available, this is by far the biggest segment of independent businesses in the United States and a target rich environment for someone that is prepared to put the time into deal development.

Note to the reader: The rest of this chapter gets into some concepts that require familiarity with business operations and financing. If you find that you are interested in the concept of purchasing a business but need help comprehending the terminology of deal making or financing, then proceed to financial command and read that chapter as well as the following chapters, and then return to this chapter with your newfound knowledge.

The following is my guide to identifying an opportunity to buy a business and getting the deal closed. The process is by no means everything you need to know about deal making and purchasing businesses. What is presented should get you comfortable with what is involved in purchasing a business, and if you're in a position where you might have the opportunity to work on a deal with a business owner, you will have the general ideas of what is involved in getting through the deal making process.

1. Looking for a company

Your best place to start is in the industry you know, and the first thought should be to the company you work at. If the business is privately held and the owner has no family interested in the business and is getting close to retirement, have a conversation with him or her about your thoughts of buying the business. Your suggestion may just be the blessing the owner has been waiting for. This type of connection has a higher chance of working out some type of seller financing getting you into the business for less.

If you're in an industry you like but don't see your current employer as a potential company you could buy, look for smaller local competitors that may be looking to sell. As noted earlier, Baby Boomers were very entrepreneurial and are now of an age where they will be open to retiring given the right deal. Better still, most smaller businesses would rather sell to an individual than to a larger competitor.

Next, talk to friends and family to look within their networks, that you are considering buying a business. Do not discount the use of social networks like Facebook as a place to post that you are looking to buy a business.

If you are serious about buying a company, this will require dedication and perseverance. To put it into perspective, Private Equity Firms that look to buy businesses for a living have a 6% close rate; that means, you need to look at as hard as 16 businesses. In the case of professionals, they look at three times that number of companies on paper to keep the funnel full on the search process.

Searchers (you'll learn more later in this section) take on average eighteen months to find a company to purchase. To be successful, you will need to be systematic and persistent to find your deal.

Location

There are two schools of thought with business location; one is that you should not limit yourself to a location and be open to looking in remote places, prepared to move to the home of the best opportunity. The other view is that you should be specific and focused with where you look so that you are not spending effort looking places that you or your family are not prepared to go.

Seeing that the type of business you're likely to buy is much smaller than what typical financial buyers search for, you should have a good mix of businesses wherever you look. If you are happy where you live, focus your search on the immediate twenty miles from your current residence. If, however, you want to move to a new location, then focus your search there.

Finally, there are several websites that post small businesses that are for sale and look to broker deals. This is a good place to do research as to how companies are valued and types of companies and deals that are being offered. I do not endorse or oppose the use of these sites; they are what they are. Just do your research to understand how the site makes money. Many are looking to broker deals and come with additional fees that will increase your cost to purchase.

In the finance world, buyers look for a proprietary deal. A proprietary deal is the deal found by the firm and is not actively being marketed. Why financial buyers like these deals is that they tend to not have competition bidding up the price of the business or brokers and investment bankers charging fees. The smaller the business, the more likely you are to find a proprietary deal.

If you choose to go through this process, be prepared for the grueling repetitive process that is involved in finding a company. On average, out of one hundred deals only twenty will deserve a deep evaluation, then only ten ever get a letter of intent, and out of those, only six will get through the due diligence process to a final deal. A six percent close rate is the average for a professional deal shop. This can be a strenuous and emotional process, as you can devote significant time to finding a business working through the deal process and then late in the game have the owner change his mind about the sale, or you find out information that makes you choose to walk away.

The larger the organization you look to purchase, the more likely there will be other suitors and an organized selling process. The real advantage is in the micro businesses that produce a good income for the owner and have the potential to grow but are too small to come up on the radar of seasoned buyers of businesses.

Depending on the industry and your personal expertise, there may also be an opportunity to partner with financial buyers that seek a seasoned expert in an industry to help them buy and grow a business in an industry. You bring the know-how, and they bring funding and operational expertise to take a good business and make it great. More on this topic later in types of buyers.

2. Valuation of a Company

When it comes to valuing a business, there is really one golden measure —cash flow. You may sometimes see the term EBITDA (earnings before interest, taxes, depreciation, and amortization); this is a proxy for a business's ability to produce cash to finance its own operations and produce a profit. In the Harvard paper on small business acquisition, the authors put forward the hypothesis that small businesses are a better value because of the low multiple applied to them. For you to evaluate a business and come up with a price, you need to understand a few things about the business and where the earnings may be hiding.

A. Seller Discretionary Earnings (SDE)

What does the current owner take out of the business each year? The seller may draw a salary, expense various benefits, and take a small profit out of the business. You will need to evaluate the total cash flow out to the owner (and family members) to understand what cash flow it produces. This is a better evaluation than EBITDA, as it demonstrates to you exactly what you, as the new owner, can pull out of the business. This is one of the benefits of being a business owner; you can run expenses through the business that are benefits to you, thereby reducing your collective tax liability. Owners can get creative, so when looking at a business, it helps to spend some time here to make sure the business really does make money and that it is what the owner thinks it is or more.

You need to validate the SDE against the owner's tax returns to assure that the numbers are solid during your due diligence (fact checking) of the business.

B. Evaluating Working Capital Needs

What kind of working capital is necessary to keep the business operating? Besides your purchase price, there needs to be capital to continue operations, and the amount of money and what working capital stays in the business will have an impact on price. For example, if the seller keeps his A/R (accounts receivable), cash, and A/P (accounts payable), the day you take over the business, you need cash on hand to begin paying bills and payroll. The cash flow must be understood to come up with your full cash needs for acquisition and operation. This evaluation needs to be done prior to making any type of offer.

3. Deal Process

There is a process to follow that leads to a successful deal being pulled together. Knowing the process will improve your confidence around deal development and provide a structure for evaluating a company and eventually providing an offer for a business.

Evaluating businesses

You will need a process to evaluate businesses first with some set criteria up front that you share with the potential seller. If your purchase of the business is contingent on the seller providing financing, then you need to be looking for businesses that the owner will be able to cash flow the repayments of owner financing and give you a wage that you can live on. If the business cannot provide the cash to fund the buyout and support you, then it is not a business

you need to spend time looking at. So, you need to know the type of deal you're looking to do along with what is negotiable and what is not. There may be some of your items that are deal killers for the seller, and the sooner this is on the table, the better.

Cash Flow/Financials

A rule of thumb is to take the seller discretionary earnings times three for a rough idea of the business value when the discretionary earnings are below $200,000. The multiple will increase as those earnings go higher.

A business with $100,000 in SDE would go for around $300,000.

When thinking about what you should expect to have saved to buy the business, a suggested guide is that 50% of the SDE over five years should pay off the principal owed to the owner (this does not include interest). In the example above, that would be:

$50,000 X 5 = 250,000. You should have $50,000 as a "cash payment" at the close of the deal.

Of course, the exact terms are between you and a seller and will be determined by the merits of the deal, but you need to be realistic about the types of businesses you are able to buy. If it's too big, you won't be able to fund the deal, and if it's too small, then you won't be able to earn enough income from the business to support yourself.

Having the framework of what type of financial structure the business needs to look like will help you to quickly assess what deals merit your further attention, and when you do look deeper, you have a context for what will work for you.

Type of Business

What are you good at or would like to do for the next ten years? The answer to that question should inform the business you look to purchase.

The best option is if you are one of the employees of a small operation where you like to work, and the owner may be looking to retire. Starting a conversation with the owner should happen after you have firmed up a plan for how you would look to acquire the business

Structuring a deal

This is by no means all that is involved in purchasing a company. You will need professional help to draw up the agreements and to make sure that you have the proper terms and conditions in place. You will need a good mergers and acquisition lawyer that has had experience with drawing up purchase sale agreements and associated documents around a small business sale. Depending on the size and complexity of the deal, expect there to be closing costs in the order of $10,000 for a simple small deal up to $100,000 for larger deals. While you may be able to defer the costs, and certainly you will want to expense them to the business as part of its formation, it is an added expense that you do need to account for in your purchase price.

Personal Equity & Seller Financing

In Financing your business, there will be detailed explanations of terms and concepts needed to determine the financing of a deal. At this early point, you need to understand that if you are pursuing acquisition to ownership, you will need to build up cash of your own to fund part or all the deal; otherwise, you will need to have other sources of capital.

One source of capital can be the seller financing the deal. When the seller finances the deal, the seller carries a promissory note signed by you to get the remaining amount due for the business plus an agreed upon interest rate to be paid over a period (typically five years). This does help the seller with tax planning and spreading income over several years, but it can be a sticking point for many sellers that have the expectation to get a cash payout and walk away.

A common term of the seller that chooses to do seller financing is a continued claim on the business assets. The loan agreement would likely demand that if you default on the loan, the owner can foreclose and reclaim the assets of the business he sold to you.

Another source of financing is commercial bank debt where a bank funds a portion of the purchase or the working capital needs of the business. This can sometimes be facilitated in deals by the seller if he has an existing relationship with a bank, and you have a relationship with the business such as long-term employment.

Outside of a note from the seller, most institutional lenders will not allow higher than a three times debt to equity ratio.

Confidentiality Agreement or Non-disclosure agreement

Anytime you look to get financials on a business or expect to have the owner share sensitive information about the way a business operates, you will need to get a CA in place. These are typically a boilerplate agreement that outlines the following:

- There will be sharing of sensitive information, and both parties will take care of it like it is their own confidential information
- There is a period that no one will share or discuss the material
- The CA does not mean there is a deal or will be a deal
- If someone breaches the agreement, there will be some type of liquidated damages determined in court

You should get a CA in place for every deal. They are a formality and can sometimes slow down the process of getting information, but are important to assure a seller that their information is safe and get them to share the data you need to determine if you want to proceed further.

Letter of Intent

When you decide to make an offer, you do so through a nonbinding letter of intent to purchase. The letter sets out the interest you have in purchasing the business.

It should be clear in the letter that you're not committing to the purchase until the due diligence is completed and a mutually agreed upon purchase sale agreement is finalized. The actual purchase happens instantaneously when you and the seller execute the purchase and sale agreement.

The Letter of intent will outline a period of exclusivity, typically ninety days, where the seller agrees to not consider other offers and allows the buyer to complete due diligence and to negotiate the final purchase and sale agreement (PSA).

This gives the buyer time to evaluate the business and make sure that all the seller's claims are true and identify any issues that could be an issue.

You will want to have a clause that provides you with the option to not complete a deal without any financial or legal obligation to the seller. The more open you have this, the better. Also steer away from any earnest money that could be lost if the deal falls through. Fifty percent of the deals that get to an LOI do not close, and you should expect to have similar results.

Term Sheet

The term sheet can be part of the Letter of Intent, or it can be a separate document. The document should lay out clearly the deal terms that you are offering. The document becomes the basis for lawyers finalizing a purchase and sale agreement. The more you can get resolved between you and the seller on the term sheet, the faster and less expensive the closing should be.

Asset Sale Vs Stock Sale

The transactions to buy most businesses is done through the purchase of all the businesses' assets, not the actual business itself. This is called an asset sale. The buyer sets up a holding company that would take ownership of the assets and do business as (DBA) the old company's name. The reason for this is, by doing so, you do not take any of the company's past liabilities along with the purchase. It creates a break between the old and new and gives the buyer protection from past liabilities.

Due diligence

This is the process of evaluating the business you look to purchase to make sure that all the representations that the owner made are true and correct. It is usually helpful to have a Certified Public Accountant (CPA) or other advisor with diligence experience to help you through the process.

Due Diligence is a critical phase of the deal process, as it is where you get to dig into the business and validate all the seller's claims as to where the business has value. It is your one shot to make sure that you're not getting a lemon. The hard part is being objective in your evaluation when so close to closing a deal and getting ownership of a business. The best deal makers I have seen are those that are unemotional, patient, and never feel any deal is a deal they must do. If your gut tells you to walk away or things are not adding up, then walk. You will find another deal.

Depending on the type of business, you may need to do detailed surveys, environmental assessments, and other types of third-party validations of the condition of assets. These costs can add up and will be yours to bear even if the deal falls through.

Purchase Sale Agreement

This is the actual contract that sets the agreement between the buyer and seller for the transaction. Usually negotiated while the seller is conducting due diligence; the contract may seem almost like a second round of negotiations.

The agreement details the transaction and will have numerous sections that break down the agreement between the parties. There will be sections covering the included and excluded assets, what liabilities are to be assumed, matters around taxes, covenants, representations and warranties, escrow, indemnifications, non-compete agreements, and how the closing and funds are to be distributed.

Reps and Warranties

The representations and warranties section details the commitments both parties make to each other. It is important for the buyer to use this section to protect against seller fraud or deception. As you and your lawyer work through this section and there is a lack of clarity around parts of the deal, you can address uncertainty with placing language in the reps and warranties section and assigning some of the purchase price to go to escrow to deal with compensation post deal once certainty can be achieved.

Escrow

Escrow is a remedy for uncertainty in the deal. A percentage of the sales price can be set aside in an escrow account to deal with and sale price adjustments that need to be made based on working capital adjustments or issues related to the representations and warranties not being met. As part of the purchase sale agreement, the terms and methods of making claims on escrow are set.

There tend to be two parts to escrow; one is for working capital adjustments, and these can go either way depending on the working capital changes that occur between the letter of intent and the close of the deal. The other portion is usually a reserve of funds to protect the buyer for unforeseen liabilities that cannot be quantified during due diligence.

Types of Buyers

There are a variety of buyers that make up the buy side of the market. You should be familiar with these types of buyers and understand how they are funded and where they typically play. This section may also provide you some other options for how you can become an owner through working with certain investors that work with entrepreneurs to buy businesses.

Individuals

Like you, there are people considering the purchase of a business as an investment and potential job. The smallest businesses are typically bought by individuals. Individual buyers typically buy one business and do so to buy a job and attain ownership. Individuals typically play in the smallest part of the market, looking for deals within twenty miles of where they live and usually find something that has an affinity with their work background. The advantage they have is, they can look at much smaller deals than financial or strategic buyers and will likely not face competitive bids.

Strategic

A strategic buyer is typically a company that is looking to expand geographically or vertically by adding complimentary services to their existing business. Strategics will look further down market (smaller companies) if they feel that the targets have a good fit for the being added on to the existing business.

These types of buyers are going to be focusing on specific geographies or niches that align with the core business growth strategy.

Financial

The scope and size of financial buyers is staggering. There is approximately 200 billion dollars a year going into private equity and 750 billion dollars of "dry powder" that is still looking to get into the market. Private equity has been very successful delivering high double digit returns, and institutional money has been focused on using PE to boost returns given publicly traded stocks and bonds have not been delving big returns. I could write a separate book just on the types and methods of private equity, so I will keep this brief and provide you some basic understanding of the different types of financial buyers and how some of these may be options for you to look at to fund your purchase of a business.

Private Equity

Is a broad category that covers everything from venture capital through traditional buyout firms. The market is growing, and as it grows, it becomes more fragmented and specialized.

The biggest segment of private equity is the buyout segment. Numerous firms have proven that getting a good manager or management team and appropriate capital can supercharge a business. Most private equity firms have some expertise that they also provide to help the companies they buy achieve success.

A private equity investment is short-lived; most firms look to get capital back in five to seven years and they have hundreds of millions of dollars of capital to deploy, so they need to invest in a portfolio of companies. While most PE firms play in the middle market, there are some that will dabble in smaller deals.

While traditional PE firms will not be interested in small deals, there are two categories of private equity that may be a particularly good fit and an option for raising funds for an acquisition.

If you are an upper manager or number two at a larger firm that does not have a succession plan for the current owner, you may have an option of bringing the deal to a PE firm to back you in a buyout. There are certain PE firms that like deals where there is a long-time manager that can continue the success of a company and bring additional capital to help the business grow and fund the exit of the owner. They would incentivize you on your performance, essentially giving you more of the company as you grow it. If you are contemplating this type of deal, understand you will not be the majority owner; the PE firm will. You will be a minority shareholder, but you will be the management of the business. If the business you are at may be a potential deal and is over three million in sales, there are likely financial buyers that will look at the business.

Search Funds

Search funds are a very interesting path to acquisition. The concept has been around since the 1980s but is widely unknown. The formation of search funds has grown significantly in the past three years as business school graduates are learning how it can provide them the opportunity of owning a business with no prior operations experience.

Most Searchers are recent graduates of business schools, with a high concentration of them coming from Stanford, Harvard, and the University of Chicago. There is a very supportive tight community at these institutions that promotes the search fund idea and brings current students, alumni, and investors together. While the norm is a searcher to be a young MBA from a top business school, the group of investors that typically participate are open to those that don't fit the mold.

Here is how a search fund works: The searcher first decides what type of search they plan to conduct. Will you be a solo searcher or a partnered search fund? The tradeoffs being if you are a solo searcher, you need to raise less money and will get more of the company you buy, but you will be on your own. Searches are lonely hard work, and some have found having a partner helpful. A partnered search can be a real advantage if the partners have complementary skills, such as one has strong financial skills and the other has industry sales experience.

As part of designing the search, the search makes choices as to the types of businesses they are looking for, the size of the business, and the possible location of the business. These choices are important, as they will be what potential investors look at and determine if they feel it is a risk they are interested in talking.

During your evaluation and design of your search, you can get excellent resources online with guides on how to put together and present a search fund to investors. Stanford, Harvard, and Chicago Booth School of Business all have excellent free resources that show you how to put together material, and there is an expectation for searchers not to deviate from the model and plagiarize material. Why, because the model has been so successful. If this is of interest to you, I suggest you start with the Sanford link below but also do further research on what local search fund resources are local to you and go to one of the meetings. This is a close and inclusive group that wants to help everyone succeed.

The next step is raising a search fund. The funds raised are for you to have a salary and costs to conduct the search for a business to buy. Typically, they raise around 450 thousand dollars to provide two years of salary and operations funding. You are expected to live on a tight budget and conserve your capital to do the search. The funds raised need to provide you with pay but also cover all your evaluation and travel costs. If the money runs out before you find your company and buy it, you're done.

The money comes from ten to twenty-five investors that buy units, with units costing from $25,000 to 50,000 each. A unit gives an investor an equity stake in the business you buy. This initial unit gets special treatment because of the risk that was taken by the investor; the first unit gets stepped up in value, usually 50%, and gives them the option to invest in the business proportionally to the units they bought. They do not have to invest in this second larger round.

This creates an interesting investment:

- You invest say $25,000 based on your belief in a person to find a good company to buy.
- You lose the money if they don't find a company, but if they do, your $25,000 becomes $37,500.
- If you like the company, the searcher found you the option to invest your portion of the purchase price, but if you don't, you have no obligation to invest.

If the searcher never finds a deal, you lose your investment in the unit, but ninety percent of funded searches find a company to buy.

For the searcher, the terms are quite standard, with them getting up to 30% of the business if they hit performance hurdles. Very few private equity firms provide this level of equity without putting cash into the deal. What is even crazier is, most of the searchers that are doing this are young MBA's that have never run a business.

Search funds have amazing success rates compared to other types of private equity. The results are not a conjecture. Stanford University has been doing research for decades on this type of investment and publish the results every three years. (Here is a link to the latest study.)

The model for success is based on: if a solid established business is transitioned to young but well trained new owner that has a good board of directors, the business will succeed.

The Search Fund Community, as it is known, is very tight knit and accessible. Most Investors have either been searchers in the past or have been doing this type of investment for decades. The firms are nationwide but tend to cluster in Boston, Chicago, and San Francisco. If this is something you're interested in exploring, here are some links to some sites of the larger search funds and investors. The investors are very active and given they tend to have inexperienced entrepreneurs, they are also focused on providing help as Board Members.

Search Fund Investors:

Pacific Lake Partners: http://www.pacificlake.com/2013-conference-videos

Anacapa Partners: http://www.anacapapartners.com/site/global/search_funds/background/

Search Fund Partners: http://www.searchfunds.net/

Operand Group: http://www.theoperandgroup.com/

The drawback to a search fund is that you are out looking for a deal and when you do get a company under LOI, you have the joy of going through a closing process while getting your investors on board for the deal. With a pool of fifteen to twenty-five investors, there will always be some that either the type of business or timing is not right and they drop out. You then should go out and find additional investors. Most deals get funded, but this creates interesting dynamics in finding and closing a deal when you are inexperienced and have no firm commitment on a funding.

Here is a link to a podcast interviewing Todd Tracy, a successful searcher:
http://www.albionfinancial.com/uploads/mediaBL_ToddTracey_HemaSource_FULL.mp3

Fundless sponsor or fundless search

This is a type of private equity that is based on the sponsor (you) going out and finding a business to buy. The best circumstances are, you are currently working at a business and have expertise in the field along with a relationship with the owner. There are a range of private equity and family offices that like to fund these types of deals.

These deals are very attractive to private equity because there is continuity in the change in ownership when it is some version of a management buyout. These are typically off-market deals that do not have an investment banker involved and no auction, so the multiple tends to be lower (a big factor in getting a good return is paying a low price).

The firms that do this type of investing also benefit from lower deal acquisition costs as sponsors, just like searchers, facilitate the process of finding companies to invest in.

These deals can be good for the sponsor because he will command a larger share of upside in the deal. You should typically negotiate three portions of earned equity: a portion that closes this is essentially your finder's fee; a portion that vests over time, and another portion that is tied to IRR of the deal for the investors.

While ownership through acquisition is not for everyone, it is one of the options that is available. It has benefits in that an existing business is easier to finance and does not have the startup risks associated with a new venture.

There is considerable legwork in finding and closing a deal, and this can be emotional. You need to have some capital and 18–24 months of determined effort to find and close a deal. There is another path to ownership that has been successful for many entrepreneurs, and we cover that next in franchising.

Franchises

Franchises have been a way to take on the role as an owner of a business without going it alone. The strength of a franchise comes from the support and structure of the franchise system. A good franchise has systematized the startup and operation of a location and supports it with training and national marketing.

The types of franchises are diverse, and it can become overwhelming evaluating all the possibilities from vending machines to service companies. Given the diversity, there will be some type of franchise that aligns with your interests and skills. Be patient and evaluate all the options.

As with buying a business, understand what you desire in this next chapter and make sure you understand the options you need. For example, if you are looking for a part-time venture to supplement your income and continue your day job that eventually can scale to a full-time opportunity, then make sure you are clear about that in your search. This is also something that fits well with some franchises and is their strength.

A good franchise system will have a proven business model associated with a national growth strategy. Unless you are an early entrant, you will be able to interview other franchisees to ask questions about the pros and cons of the group and be able to get mentoring from other franchise owners; they bring you knowledge and a sense of community.

There are drawbacks. Franchises are highly regulated by state and federal government as well as by the franchisor. Agreements can be one sided and limit your options around what you can do with your business. I have had more than one person I have worked with have issues with either buying or selling an existing franchise.

Another big drawback is with fee structures. Most franchises have a gross revenue fee that they charge, and if the business comes with significant fixed costs, you can feel some real pain if sales drop, and you get squeezed between the fixed costs and the post fee revenues.

Today there is a range of price points and business models to choose from when looking at owning and operating a franchise. A good place to start is looking at Entrepreneur magazine's top 500 list of franchises to see the best of the best and to get a feel for the breadth of options.

What to look for in a franchise:

¥ A franchise where there are still substantial growth opportunities yet old enough that you can research on how they work with franchisees over time.

- Understand the true initial investment and ongoing economics. Part of the franchise model is ongoing royalties that are paid to the chain, and this impacts your profitability.
- One that has not recently had a change in ownership or management. Understanding the management style of the franchiser and how they interact with franchisees is important.
- Understand how they support location choices and start up support. While the brand may be looking to expansion and getting more location pins in the map at HQ, you will be on the front line and without good support, or worse, with a bad location, your business will suffer.
- Do a deep dive into the overall franchises financials and how it generates revenues. Many franchises get start up fees, cuts of gross revenues, and make a margin on supplies sold to the franchisee.

Remember, they are a sales organization; evaluate all the claims made and do your homework. The chain is focused on getting locations to open, and if they are using other sellers, they have their own agenda that they are focused on achieving. An example is if you are contacted by franchise marketer; this individual will look to fit you in two to three franchises that they feel are the right fit for you.

Make sure you understand the Franchisors Disclosure Document (FDD); the document is required to be supplied to you by the franchisor, and there is minimum time period you are required to have to review this document prior to signing a contract. It is also worth your time reviewing if there are any pending actions being reviewed by the federal trade commission as well as State franchise regulators.

Here is a link to the FTC's documents:

https://www.ftc.gov/tips-advice/business-center/guidance/consumers-guide-buying-franchise

In summary, franchises can be an excellent option for starting a business that has established systems to support it. Franchises also offer a diverse range of options to meet customer needs and niches that can align with what your interests are.

STARTUP

When you hear the word startup, what comes to mind?

Is it the tech start-up with angel investors, venture capital, B and C rounds on the way to be the next unicorn IPO, or is it a home-based side hustle that will grow into enough income for you to have the lifestyle you dream of?

Maybe something in the middle? This is where most of us land.

Regardless of the type of startup you are thinking about, this book will, in the long run, be helpful to operating any business successfully. Looking to launch a start-up that will seek funding from others? Guess what, your chances of raising cash are higher when you can demonstrate your plan to create a return for those investors.

Keep in mind a lot has changed in the world of venture capital. There have been too many dollars chasing investments, and all the seed funds and accelerators have data and now see that the ratio of duds to sky rockets has left them with poor returns. I bring this up because if you are going to live in a world of venture funding, applying the concepts in this book will differentiate you from the pack.

I will spend the rest of this section focused on the path of the traditional bootstrap start-up, where you go out on your own (or with partners) to build a business from scratch. The business can be anything from being an independent truck driver to selling a product or service. Like most new businesses, you will start alone with an idea and maybe a customer or two look to create value out of your sweat.

Earlier, we discussed the options around buying an existing business or franchise as a way to get into the owner's chair, but if you are inspired to go out on your own in support of what you feel, you need to get a level set on how you're starting your startup. Reading this book first shows you are doing your research and this research with some audacious action will result in a successful business.

Ways to get started

There are, in my opinion, two main ways an individual that is looking to start up a business on their own get going. They are the part time side hustle and the grand plan. The difference is not in the commitment but in what is best suited for risk reduction and success. Let's go through both.

Starting with a side hustle.

Getting started before you leave your day job can be a great way to test your idea and still have a safety net. Clay Collins of Leadpages talks about finding your minimal viable audience, and this may be something that you should do before you take the plunge of quitting your day job. It is a great way to test and perfect your offering as well as determine how enthusiastic you are to do this work on an ongoing basis. Later, I cover in the <u>online presence</u> section ways to do this with a very professional presentation but at a low cost and from your home. I will outline tools to build out your business as well as discuss existing platforms that are good sources for business. Think about this: ten years ago, for you to sell a book, you needed to get a publishing deal. Today, you can easily publish that book on an online platform, and you can bring to the market a high-quality product by accessing excellent editors, cover illustrators, and other support staff via platforms like Fiverr. This example shows how you can get started as an author or a proofreader and build a good business that is global without leaving your house.

Freelancing, online retail, and independent publishing are all scalable ventures today that you can start out small and test the market and with some simple planning, you can structure a path to growing a business with very little capital. The trick is, right from the start, you treat the first dollar of your capital like it is coming from your alter ego, the venture capitalist, and expect that dollar to come back with more dollars just like it, not less.

This also removes the excuses of capital and time. You can start small working in the free time you have and see the results, learn from them, and adapt.

Grander Plans

As your plans grow in complexity and grandeur, so does your need for capital and time. This statement in not meant to be discouraging; rather, pointing out the need for a solid plan of execution. Remember, any good investor needs to see a plan to evaluate the risk; since your alter ego is a great investor, you need to put the plan together that shows the plan along with capital needs and expected returns. This can be a few pages. In fact, I believe that a one-page business plan can be enough if part of that page has twelve to eighteen months of budgeting for the plan.

INCORPORATION

SHOULD I INCORPORATE?

As an artist, author, freelancer, contractor, or individual who has a cottage business, you may have asked yourself: Is there an advantage to incorporating my business?

First off, you may not be aware that the state or county where your business is based likely has requirements regarding registering to transact business—even if you are operating your business as a sole proprietor under your own name. For example, if you were running your business as John Smith Attorney at Law, your state or county may require you to place a printed advertisement for a certain period of time and legally register your business name. These laws were put in place a long time ago to protect the public from shady operators and to protect you in case another business tries to use your business's name.

To determine the best course of action, you will need to analyze and understand the types of entities of incorporation and the benefits and the drawbacks of each. If your business operates in multiple states, you'll also need to assess the rules each state has for incorporation to select the right one for establishing your company's charter to determine the optimal one for you and the best State to provide your company charter.

A Snippet of the History of Corporations

Corporations are a rather new concept; historically, they were much less common than they are today. Through the 19th century, chartering a corporation required a legislative act by a state. One Example: In 1809, Robert Fulton and Robert Livingston were given a charter by the legislature of New Your state for exclusive navigation of the waters of New York by Steam Ships. The charter established a monopoly for Fulton and his partners; he eventually sought similar monopolies for other states. The New York Corporate Charter set in motion a course of events that resulted in a landmark Supreme Court decision, Gibbons v. Ogden asserting the federal government's authority to regulate interstate commerce and setting the foundation for competition between businesses.

In 1882, Samuel C. Dodd, the General Solicitor (head attorney) for Standard Oil, organized the company as a Trust to pool the organization's resources and control its complex network of interests. He created the modern corporation. Later, this organization was rolled up under a New Jersey state charter as the Standard Oil Company. The huge monopolies of the 19th and early 20th centuries — like Standard Oil, Carnegie Steel, and the railroads of Cornelius Vanderbilt — set in place structures that allowed the birth of the global corporation and the ability for companies to seek outside capital from private and public sources.

Over time, the trust and corporation laws have been revised or instituted to fill the growing need for legal structures to organize and control businesses. Today, every state has an office that deals with the incorporation of companies, and most states offer a range of corporate entities types to suit the needs of U.S. businesses.

Where Do I Start?

First, read through this guide to learn about the types of corporate structures and the pros and cons of each. Next, if your business operates in multiple states, read the section Location of Incorporation and do your research on the incorporation requirements of those states you plan to do business to determine the best one for you.

Once you're comfortable with the notion that incorporation is right for your company, use the handy checklist at the back of the book to work your way through the steps of incorporating your business.

When Should I Incorporate?

If your venture currently meets the following criteria or will in the next twelve months, then incorporation will make sense.

- Will you have investors in the business or multiple owners?
- Will your business have over $10,000 in sale?
- Will your business generate over $5,000 of profit?
- Will you get credit from vendors for inventory?
- Will you be selling a product or service that exposes you to a product liability claim?

If you say yes to any of the above, I suggest looking at incorporating. A small hobby business with little income may not make sense to formally incorporate, given you will have costs associated with filing for the corporation and filing another tax return. State filing fees run around one hundred to three hundred dollars. Your new corporation will require a tax return even if all the income passes through to you. Think through these costs and make sure that the business can support the additional expenses you will have with incorporation.

Location of Incorporation

Location, location, location. States provide incorporation, so you must select one or more for your company. For most businesses, you will need only one entity (and as we will cover later, you can get your entity qualified to do business in other states), but more complex businesses may have multiple entities in multiple States.

One of my start-ups was headquartered in Illinois but operated in Wyoming. We had a very complicated corporate structure to support investor protection, operations across multiples states, and environmental liability protection.

Investors were members of a Delaware limited liability company (LLC) that acted as a holding company. The company did not operate as a traditional business; it only held the stock of the operating company and had membership interests that were helped by investors.

The holding company was the sole member of an Illinois LLC. The Illinois company was the operating company where we conducted the day-to-day operations of the business. To do business in Wyoming, North Dakota, and Texas, we had the Illinois LLC qualified to do business in each of those states.

At every one of our physical locations, we set up a separate Wyoming limited liability corporation; the assets for the location were owned by each individual company with the owner of the company being the Illinois service company, as the only member of the five Wyoming LLCs. The reasoning behind this structure was that if there was an issue of personal injury or environmental liability on the site, the other locations would be protected from claims.

The Illinois LLC also was the sole shareholder of an Illinois Corporation that employed all staff. The C Corporation allowed us to provide W-2s to equity holding managers, something you cannot do in an LLC.

The Illinois Corporation was also qualified to do business in Wyoming and Texas.

Now, this was a complicated business that was asset intensive and had safety and environmental risks that we looked to compartmentalize. We spent several thousand dollars a year in fees to maintain this structure. It made sense for the business, based on the size and the work we were doing. By no means do you need this level of complexity for your small business. I share the example to demonstrate how corporate organization can be used to protect investors and various parts of a business from potential liabilities as well as help to give an organizing structure that complies with state and federal law.

So where do you start?

My opinion is incorporate in your home state. A company located where you live and pay taxes is simple. Certainly, if you are the only employee and you do most of your work and reside in that state, then your choice of where to incorporate is simple. If you begin to have significant recurring sales in another State or plan to open an office, you can then choose to get your company qualified to do business in that state or set up a subsidiary in that State.

Most states require a local address for your corporate entity. That means if you set up in a state you do not reside in, and you don't have an office in that State, you will need to go through an agent that acts on your behalf in that State.

You may have heard about Nevada and Wyoming as states that have special limited liability companies that offer added protections for your assets. While they might make it harder for someone to identify you as the owner and have some variation in corporate laws from your home State, they won't protect you if you break the law by hiding assets or shirk tax liabilities. A determined tax agent will eventually find them and you.

Delaware is also a very common location to incorporate a business. The state laws are favorable to companies and corporate protection. The "First State" is an excellent choice if you are planning to go national and take other people's money for investment. If this is the case, I suggest you speak to a lawyer familiar with corporate structuring to help set up the appropriate structures and provide the necessary documents (i.e., Operating Agreement, Private Placement Memorandum). Doing this right the first time will bring credibility when you are out raising money and when investors begin doing diligence on your company.

The Wind Up

1. Look to your state of residence as the state to incorporate your business.
2. Complex businesses may require complex structures.
3. If you plan to fundraise or seek venture capital, the state of

Delaware may be a good choice based on the comfort that professional investors have with the chancery laws.

Determine the Best Type of Structure

Types are:

- Sole Proprietor
- Limited Liability Company LLC
- Corporation Sub Chapter C or S
- Limited Liability Partnership LLP

Sole Proprietor

Whether you register or not, you are a sole proprietor in the eyes of Uncle Sam if you sell four hundred dollars or more on your own. You are expected by the IRS to claim the income on your personal income tax. It is likely that there are county and state regulations to registering as a sole proprietor to legally do business.

DBA Doing Business As

If you plan to do business under another name "Doing Business As" (DBA), you need to register your business name and advertise that you will be doing business under an assumed name.

You will need to record the Business with the state or county to conduct business. In Illinois, if you are a sole proprietor/ individual and looking to register a name to do business under you, register with the county clerk

, or if you are seeking to do business under another name (DBA), you will need to register that name with the same Clerk. The fee runs around $50-110.

You will need:

- Registration with County or State
- Advertising your DBA for one month in approved newspapers

Your registration protects you from others using the name.

Limited Liability Company (LLC)

A limited liability corporation provides an independent entity. It provides flexibility with how you want the membership to work, share profits, and operate. All the ins and outs should be documented in an operating agreement. You don't need an operating agreement if you are a single member LLC or two members that are husband and wife.

The liability that is limited is your obligation for debts incurred by the LLC. Unsecured debtors have limited recourse if your LLC goes bankrupt. A note of caution: if you personally guarantee loans for the LLC, you will have the liability, so beware.

In an LLC, all profits get passed through to partners. Profits will be taxed at the member's personal income tax rate and will need to include self-employment taxes. Be sure to allocate the cash to pay the taxes. If you reinvest the profits, and there is no cash, you will have to reach into your pocket to pay the taxes. *See more in the taxes section of Business owner's Compendium.*

Operating Agreement

If you have multiple members, you need to have an operating agreement. I guarantee if you don't, you and your partners will be at odds with how to distribute profits or who has certain rights over others. Operating Agreements are also important in situations where one partner is passive and may be contributing capital, and the other partner is more active and contributing less capital. Hash out the details before the profits roll in.

Articles of Incorporation

Articles of Incorporation are a simple document from the state that shows that the business is incorporated, the type of incorporation, and the purpose of the firm.

Annual Registration

A state requires a renewal fee and a filing to keep records up to date and your LLC in good standing. If you do not do so, the state will cancel the charter, and the entity will no longer exist, losing all the protections that it provides.

If you choose to close an LLC, be sure to file a final return and to file with the state that you are suspending the charter.

CORPORATION C & S

Some differences on Corporations. First Corporations pay a corporate tax rate on profits unless the Corporation is Subchapter S. Corporate taxes create a double taxation where there are taxes paid on corporate profits, and then again by shareholders on dividends.

Corporations also have stricter rules around distribution on profits. Retained Profits increase shareholder equity equally, and profits that are distributed go out as dividends. The Profit is split equally across the shareholders of the same types of stock. There can be different stock classes that have various rights and payment priority, but in the case of a company with just common stock, dividends are split equally among those shareholders.

One benefit is that a corporation can employ owners. You can draw a salary and be treated like any other employee.

If you elect to have your corporation set up as a subchapter S, then the company's profits flow to the shareholder's tax returns. There are limits to the number of shareholders (100) and who can be shareholders when you can elect to be a subchapter S.

As an S corp, you get the ability to collect a salary with a W-2. An advantage if you are self-employed, as it becomes difficult to qualify for car loans and home mortgages when you are self-employed. As a W-2 employee, that little piece of paper ticks the right boxes for most lenders.

Once your company is making money, you have some added tax advantages (within reason) as a self-employed single employee in an S corp. You can optimize your salary level and profits to lessen your tax burden.

By setting a lower salary that accrues lower payroll taxes and allowing the rest flow out as profits that do not attract payroll taxes like an LLC, you will have a lower overall tax burden and eliminate the second taxation on profits. Be careful; for decades, many have thought they would play games and run small salaries to keep the payroll taxes down. The taxing authorities at the State and Federal level have seen this and every other trick and can fine you and collect back taxes on what they determine should have been salary. A rule of thumb is: your salary should run at levels paid to a non-owner doing the same role or 50% of the company's profits. As the single employee in the early days, 50% of the profits may not cover a month of your mortgage, but you are setting the habit of paying yourself. Later, when your company makes a million dollars a year, a $500,000 salary may be excessive for the role, but it is an easy sell to the tax man as appropriate given the level of profits.

By-laws

Your Corporation must have by-laws that deal with the election of the board, shareholder rights, and frequency of board meetings. Most States require board minutes and an annual report filed with the State. The annual report will have limited disclosure requirements with a focus on who is on the Board.

To elect to be a Sub Chapter S, you are required to fill out a form with the IRS. I suggest you do this immediately:

https://www.irs.gov/pub/irs-pdf/f2553.pdf

BENEFIT CORPORATIONS or B Corp

This legal classification falls along the same lines as an S Corp, C Corp, or limited liability company. Twenty-seven states and the District of Columbia recognize and charter benefit corporations. Benefit corporations function almost identically to S and C Corps, with two differences:

1. The corporate charter must include social good.

2. A benefit corporation must comply with a third-party standard that measures corporate social responsibility.

This does not create a tax-exempt certification, and the business is required to pay appropriate taxes on profits. What is different is that there is clarity around the social or environmental benefit of the company and that this social benefit may take precedence to the profit motive of most firms.

CERTIFIED B CORPS

This is a certification awarded to businesses that pass B Lab's social responsibility assessment. Certified B Corps must retake the assessment every two years, and each year, 10 percent of certified B Corps are audited in person.

Limited Liability Partnership LLP

Some States have LLPs for Professional Partnerships (i.e., Lawyers, Engineers, Accountants). The corporation is also used sometimes for Investment firms that are doing venture capital or Private Equity.

Qualification

Most states have a process and fee for getting foreign corporations qualified to do business in the state. Typically, you need to fill out a form, pay a filing fee, and provide a certificate of good standing from the State where the entity is chartered. Most sites allow for you to do this all electronically, although there are others that require you to wait before doing business until your qualification is approved.

File and Pay Fees

When it comes to filing, you can do this a couple of different ways. I believe if you are running a small business that you are the only employee, you should do it yourself and save the money that it would cost to have someone else do it. Here are the options:

Lawyer

You can hire a lawyer that will file the appropriate documents. You will pay the filing fees and for his or an assistant's time to file.

Web Service

There are dozens of sites that will incorporate your business; they are for-profit businesses, and there will be additional charges along with the filing fees. In some cases, they can also act as an agent if you are out of state.

Filing Agencies

There are still brick and mortar facilities that will do the filing for you and act as the agent for your business if you need this service.

DYI

If you are a single member or a husband-wife relationship where a partnership agreement is not going to be put in place, you can set up the entity yourself. I have done this several times as well as dealing with all the renewals and filings for my LLC. In most states, this can be done online, and you will get your articles of incorporation in less than 48 hours.

Links to sites: Here are links to State websites where you can electronically file for incorporation; they are all direct to the State regulator that handles registration for that State. I am not recommending these above others; you can always use other sites, but they will typically charge a fee above the filing fee.

Alabama: https://www.alabamainteractive.org/sos/welcome.action

Alaska: https://www.commerce.alaska.gov/web/cbpl/Corporations.aspx

Arizona: https://www.azsos.gov/business/corporations

Arkansas: http://www.sos.arkansas.gov/BCS/Pages/default.aspx

California: http://www.sos.ca.gov/business-programs/business-entities/forms/

Colorado: http://www.sos.state.co.us/pubs/business/businessHome.html

Connecticut: http://www.sots.ct.gov/sots/cwp/view.asp?a=3172&q=525434

Delaware: http://corp.delaware.gov/index.shtml

Florida: http://dos.myflorida.com/sunbiz/

Georgia: https://ecorp.sos.ga.gov/

Hawaii: https://portal.ehawaii.gov/business/starting-a-business/

Idaho: https://sos.idaho.gov/corp/index.html

Illinois: http://www.cyberdriveillinois.com/services/business.html

Indiana: http://www.in.gov/sos/business/index.htm

Iowa: https://sos.iowa.gov/business/FormsAndFees.html

Kansas: https://www.sos.ks.gov/business/business.html

Kentucky: https://app.sos.ky.gov/ftsearch/

Louisiana: http://www.sos.la.gov/BusinessServices/StartABusiness/Pages/default.aspx

Maine: http://www.maine.gov/sos/cec/corp/

Maryland: https://egov.maryland.gov/businessexpress

Massachusetts: https://www.sec.state.ma.us/cor/

Michigan: http://www.michigan.gov/lara/0,4601,7-154-61343---,00.html

Minnesota: http://www.sos.state.mn.us/business-liens/start-a-business/

Mississippi: http://www.sos.ms.gov/BusinessServices/Pages/default.aspx

Missouri: https://www.sos.mo.gov/business/corporations

Montana: http://sos.mt.gov/business/

Nebraska: http://www.sos.ne.gov/business/corp_serv/

Nevada: https://nvsos.gov/index.aspx?page=4

New Hampshire: http://sos.nh.gov/Corp_Div.aspx

New Jersey: http://www.nj.gov/njbusiness/

New Mexico: http://www.sos.state.nm.us/Business_Services/Corporations_Overview.aspx

New York: https://www.dos.ny.gov/corps/

North Carolina: https://www.sosnc.gov/corporations/printforms.aspx

North Dakota: http://sos.nd.gov/business/business-services

Ohio: https://bsportal.sos.state.oh.us/(S(4zle1nb34hcmmyukqqahpoel))/default.aspx

Oklahoma: https://www.sos.ok.gov/(S(hfi1b155qdirny45spx-epd45))/business/default.aspx

Oregon: http://sos.oregon.gov/business/Pages/default.aspx

Pennsylvania: http://www.dos.pa.gov/BusinessCharities/Business/Pages/default.aspx

Rhode Island: http://sos.ri.gov/divisions/business-portal

South Carolina: http://www.scsos.com/business_filings

South Dakota: https://sosenterprise.sd.gov/businessservices/

Tennessee: http://sos.tn.gov/business-services

Texas: http://www.sos.state.tx.us/corp/index.shtml

Utah: http://corporations.utah.gov/business/

Vermont: https://www.sec.state.vt.us/corporationsbusiness-services.aspx

Virginia: https://www.scc.virginia.gov/clk/

Washington: https://www.sos.wa.gov/corps/

West Virginia: http://apps.sos.wv.gov/business/corporations/

Wisconsin: https://www.wdfi.org/corporations/

Wyoming: https://wyobiz.wy.gov/Business/Default.aspx

Tax ID Number: Once you have your articles of incorporation, you can set up your Employer Identification Number (EIN). Think of it as your corporation's social security number. You can apply for this online, and it is free. You will need it for filing returns and

IRS: https://www.irs.gov/businesses/small-businesses-self-employed/apply-for-an-employer-identification-number-ein-online

Check List:

1. Have a company name: Make sure you're happy with it because you will pay a fee to change it later

2. Have an office address for your company

3. Have details on Managing Members or Board Members, including social security numbers and home address for the filing

4. Select the State of Incorporation

5. Research that State's options for entities

6. Have a credit card if you plan to file online

7. Select an LLC, Corporation, or LLP

8. Save your Articles of Incorporation

9. Get and EIN number from the IRS

10. Make your dreams come true

PART TWO

RUNNING A BUSINESS

FINANCIAL COMMAND

BANK ACCOUNT

Many small businesses operate out of a bank account on a cash basis for accounting purposes. If you are running a small home based business, then there is nothing wrong with this. The only suggestion is that you keep the business accounts separate from your personal assets. Co-mingling funds and assets can set a bad precedent. If you have gone through the process of incorporating your business, then you need to have a separate account for the business. Working out of your personal account can lead to tax issues or provide evidence to creditors that your business assets and personal assets are not separate and giving them the grounds to pursue your personal assets in the case of a bankruptcy.

When do you open an account solely for your business? My suggestion is: the sooner, the better. Getting your personal and business funds separate is the most important part of fencing off your affairs.

As soon as possible, differentiate funds while you and your business are in some respects one in the same; you need to clearly delineate your cash that goes into the business as equity and loans and what cash is coming out as payroll, distributions, equity, interest, or principal. All this impacts your accounting practices and your tax liabilities. As time goes by, how money has gone in and comes out can have significant tax implications and impact your return.

The key items to think about:

- Bank Fees - Depending on your bank, you can end up burning up a bunch of your cash on fees. As a percentage, it could be very high compared to the business income. This can be addressed by setting up a second personal account rather than a business account to evade business account fees or minimum balances.

- If you are setting up a business account, this usually means you need to formalize your business with a DBA filing or corporation. After 9/11, banks have tight regulations on assuring who owns an account. So in the early days, you may have to get a separate account in your own name to run the business from but can convert this once you're free or you are of a size to incorporate and then have the appropriate documents to get a corporate bank account.

- You should always set up a checking account and a savings account. You will need an account to stash away cash that is needed for quarterly payments.

Financials

The level of financials you need to keep is a function of what you are trying to achieve. If you are planning to go and raise 10 million dollars to do a start-up, then you will need to have financial models and projections that show sources and uses of cash for the next five years. If you are just running a cottage business that is just starting and the income you get from there is small and irregular, then you can do all your work on your personal tax return and check book. Most businesses are somewhere in the middle, and there needs to be regular accounting, and you, as the owner, need to be able to use your financials to help you guide your business where you want it to go.

Why do you need Financials?

Keeping monthly financials has two significant benefits:

◆ You reduce the work and cost of doing taxes at the end of the year by keeping records current rather than trying.

◆ Accurate monthly financials will help you to see how your business is progressing and provide you with an indication as to where you need to work on your business.

This section will not get into double entry accounting and the nuances of ledgers. The objective is not to turn you into a bookkeeper but to highlight the need for tracking your business performance and having records so that you can provide yourself with reliable statements to know the condition of your business.

Excel/Numbers/Google Docs based accounting

As mentioned for smaller operations, this is a good place to track sales and costs. I use excel because I am a heavy Excel user and build complex models but for simple accounting excel, numbers open office or google docs are all great options.

If you go to the free data room, you will find copies of some income statements you can use. The income statement.xls is an example you can work with. If you have an accountant you work with, he or she may also have a spreadsheet that you can work with. I would suggest using the form they have developed if they prepare taxes for you. The statement will be in a format they are comfortable with, and using that form should result in them spending less time on your taxes at the end of the year.

Regardless of the form you use, the idea here is to capture your monthly numbers and getting into the habit of looking at your statements monthly, even if it is just the act of putting them together. Over time, you will have a valuable tool for comparing past and current performance.

You also will need to have statements to determine your taxes. You are required to make quarterly payments for the business or for your personal tax liability where the tax liability passes through to your personal tax return. Not doing so will result in penalties and interest at the end of the year.

Accounting Systems

Given the type of business you are running, you can decide when you need to start using an accounting system and moving beyond spreadsheet tracking of your business. I have lived in these worlds from had experience from my own spreadsheets for simple businesses, various cloud-based solutions, and a couple of office-based networked ERP systems.

If you are less than ten transactions a month and below $15,000 a year in sales, you can do this work on a spreadsheet and save costs. There are some cloud-based programs that offer free but typically have a hook tied to the number of transactions or reconciling to accounts. The key objective is to have a statement that allows you to keep an eye on your business and captures your transactions so you can file your taxes on a quarterly basis. Doing this work monthly or as part of your weekly schedule will save you the distraction and overwhelming feeling at year end when you need to get your tax information together.

Cloud Based Accounting Systems

90% of businesses can be run from a cloud based accounting package. The one I have used the most is QuickBooks. It scales well and has an assortment of add-ons to customize it to your needs. This gets you an accounting package for around $600 a year without payroll services.

There is also a half dozen other programs out there that are all decent.

The big weakness I have seen with QuickBooks online is that it's light on dealing with bills of materials and manufacturing.

ERP Systems

Of course, even these are now moving to the cloud, but an enterprise resource planning system typically has a workflow and business front end that all rolls up to a general ledger for the accountants. It can include HR and sophisticated planning and purchasing systems for specific industries.

The takeaway on accounting systems that I can give you is, once you are at a point where your business dictates the need, then look to do so with a subscription to a cloud-based system. The more complex you go, the higher your ongoing costs will be, and you will have a significant distraction for serving your customer while you bog down with a software integration at the end of the year.

Regardless of the form you use, the idea here is to capture your monthly numbers and getting into the habit of looking at your statements monthly, even if it is the act of putting them.

Look at the software you use and make sure that the accounting you select is compatible. If your business is a growing Shopify site, then you want to make sure that the accounting is compatible with a simple API token or add-on software so that you don't find yourself needing to customize some connection.

Various Cloud Accounting Packages that are cloud based and work well for small businesses.

Freshbooks

sage

Xero

QuickBooks

Cash Rules Everything Around Me.

—Wu Tang Clan

Money isn't everything but it ranks right up there with oxygen.

—Zig Zigler

CASH FLOW

You have heard it before, "Cash is king." It is. It will tell you what you can and can't do or if you will be in business tomorrow.

As an early stage entrepreneur or someone looking to quit your day job, you know that the lack of cash can be a limiting factor for you achieving your goals. Even well-funded startups need to be watching cash, because if they are not, the investors are and will take control if they feel cash is not utilized effectively.

THEORETICAL

Cash Flow: the amount of cash moving in and out of a business in each period.

The Basics of Cash Flow

Cash In - Cash out = Free Cash

Cash out = Tax Payments/liabilities + Pay + Expenses + Capital Reserves

Positive Cash Flow indicates that through the operation of your business, you produce extra cash from the operation than it costs to run it.

Negative Cash flow indicates your operations use up more cash than they generate. If this does not change, you will need more capital to keep going, or you will go out of business. This is sometimes noted as a burn rate, meaning that your business burns up cash by its operations.

Cash Flow Neutral is a term typically used when navigating troubled water—as in, after the loss of our biggest customer, I could adjust and get the business cash flow neutral in three months. In troubled times, the best we can hope for as a short-term goal is being cash flow neutral. The state of neutral cash flow for a business is that it is not creating more cash but can continue operations if the state of the business remains steady.

<u>Cash Collection Cycle:</u> Your business uses cash, and then collects cash—and this takes time. If you extend credit to your clients, the collection cycle can be extended by days or months. It is important for you to quantify the average collection period and organize your business around this cycle.

Your objective is to get your business to cash flow positive as fast as possible with the shortest cash collection cycle. The shorter the time it takes your cash to go out and find some other cash and bring it back home, the faster you can grow your business.

Cash Flow is the single best indicator of the performance of your business. You need to be able to characterize the amount, charge (positive or Negative), and its timeliness. An operation gets into trouble, and the owners feel helpless and overwhelmed when there are issues with negative cash flow or low positive cash flow that is untimely.

Timing issues with cash flow:

If you find that you have low positive cash flow and your time to collect that cash is long, your ability to build a cash reserve, AKA working capital pool, takes time and thereby slows your ability to grow the business.

Cash flow timing is particularly important in bootstrap situations, as your ability to generate cash is the sole source of funds for new growth initiatives.

Timing is the source of the problem and solution to cash gaps. Cash gaps appear when you need to disburse cash but have not been paid yet. Cash flow timing will impact your credit with vendors or can potentially hold up your ability to continue operations if you are stuck waiting on a client payment to pay your suppliers.

I chose to lead the financial section with cash flow rather than the income statement because cash is that important. Understanding your cash flow and making it the focus of your business may be the single most important thing you can do as a business owner, because if you run out of cash, you're out of business.

If you are running a smaller operation and working from a check book and contemplating the use of an income statement, then it makes sense to begin talking about cash flow because you have been running your business on a Cash Basis, and you need to understand the difference in cash basis, cash flow, and accrual.

If you're not aware of these differences, an income statement can give you a false sense of security about performance. More on this later in the Income Statement section.

Conserving cash, knowing where cash is and when it is going to be in your account is the single most important preoccupation you should have, as it is the best temperature for the health and hardiness of your enterprise. Cash flow is also the key determinant of the value of a business. The more cash your business spins off, the higher price someone would pay for it. Now you can see getting a business with a strong cash flow focus helps to keep you out of trouble and creates more value if you choose to exit.

Managing your cash properly is the most important thing you can do to monitor and mitigate risk in your business. Most businesses fail because they run out of cash, and most business owners that get in trouble with the IRS—it is, again, because they didn't manage their cash properly and used cash that should be held for taxes or to pay for other expenses. Never do this—Ever!

You will need a tool for helping you to manage your cash flow. If you are familiar with a Statement of Cash Flows, you may cringe and wonder how that will help. If you are not familiar with one, below is a cash flow statement from Alphabet Inc., the holding company for Google, lifted from the March 31, 2016, 10-Q. Prepare to cringe.

Alphabet Inc.
CONSOLIDATED STATEMENTS OF CASH FLOWS
(In millions)

	Three Months Ended March 31,	
	2018	2019
	(unaudited)	
Operating activities		
Net income	$ 3,515	$ 4,267
Adjustments:		
Depreciation and impairment of property and equipment	938	1,156
Amortization and impairment of intangible assets	239	216
Stock-based compensation expense	1,203	1,494
Deferred income taxes	71	414
Loss on marketable and non-marketable investments, net	16	280
Other	61	64
Changes in assets and liabilities, net of effects of acquisitions:		
Accounts receivable	696	818
Income taxes, net	827	271
Prepaid revenue share, expenses and other assets	43	185
Accounts payable	(24)	(259)
Accrued expenses and other liabilities	(801)	(1,064)
Accrued revenue share	(205)	(131)
Deferred revenue	(59)	18
Net cash provided by operating activities	6,722	7,658
Investing activities		
Purchases of property and equipment	(2,927)	(2,428)
Purchases of marketable securities	(12,556)	(20,748)
Maturities and sales of marketable securities	10,389	17,443
Purchases of non-marketable investments	(1,074)	(321)
Cash collateral related to securities lending	(1,120)	(257)
Investments in reverse repurchase agreements	50	100
Acquisitions, net of cash acquired, and purchases of intangible assets	(94)	(34)
Net cash used in investing activities	(7,304)	(6,245)
Financing activities		
Net payments related to stock-based award activities	(493)	(857)
Repurchases of capital stock	0	(2,098)
Proceeds from issuance of debt, net of costs	3,305	3,956
Repayments of debt	(3,308)	(3,952)
Net cash used in financing activities	(496)	(2,911)
Effect of exchange rate changes on cash and cash equivalents	(293)	60
Net decrease in cash and cash equivalents	(1,371)	(1,438)
Cash and cash equivalents at beginning of period	16,347	16,549
Cash and cash equivalents at end of period	$ 14,976	$ 15,111

What you are looking at is a cash flow statement using the indirect method. You may be wondering, *What the hell good would this do me?* Or *I sure the hell don't understand what that's all about.* That's OK because the real purpose of this document is in reconciling an Income Statement to a

Balance Sheet and show how changes to the two statements impact cash. It is a lousy tool for managing the day-to-day cash of a business.

It is also likely that you also don't have sixteen billion dollars of cash and cash equivalents sitting around like Alphabet does, so your cash reserves are very tight (or non-existent) and require far more attention.

You need to understand the impact of cash flow on your business and how to track it on a regular basis.

PRACTICAL

Managing Cash Flow

Pick a day each week that you will review your cash flow. Sunday night before the week kicks off if you typically are out of the office or maybe every Thursday. It does not matter but put on your calendar at least an hour each week where you review and update your cash flow. As your business grows, you will likely need more time than an hour, as you will also coordinate paying bills and transferring funds as part of updating your cash flow.

Cash In

The proceeds from your business are the cash in. You need a method of tracking the amount and time when the cash comes in.

Cash Out

Expenses

You need to track the amount and when they are paid. In a small business, you may be using your credit card as a means of managing cash, so monthly list the itemized expenses and the payment to the credit card company in such a way as to not the actual cash going out but also what that cash was used to pay. If you have suppliers that extend you credit, I suggest you pick certain dates to pay all the bills. This becomes part of your cash flow review process, and you can select to pay only once a month or two times a month, but if you are the sole employee, then keep this limited to twice a month. If you coordinate it so you do not get past due with those who have extended credit, you can keep it to once a month.

Pay

We will talk about owner pay later in the book, but you need to be moving a portion of the income out to you.

Taxes

Every time you sell something, you create a tax liability. The IRS expects you to pay them on a quarterly basis. This means that you need to allocate a portion of your revenue, hold it for a period of time, and then cut a check to the US treasury and maybe your State Treasurer. There will be more on this in the taxes section, but the key point now is to allocate the portion of taxes you need to pay in the future and set them aside, and then pay them when they are due.

You can track this however you want. If you have a hobby business, this could all be done on one sheet of paper. For businesses that are larger or growing, a 52-week cash flow is an indispensable tool.

Fifty-two-week cash flow

I like to use a tool called the 52-week cash flow to track the ins and outs of cash and to provide insight to you about your growing or shrinking cash balance. Having advanced notice that your cash flows are shrinking gives you time to figure out why and adjust your operations before the business finds itself out of cash. You can find the spreadsheet at the following link.

Don't be overwhelmed by the fifty-two weeks. You're not going to put in all fifty-two weeks at once; that is too hard and impossible to project at the start. You start with the current calendar week that you are in when you start doing this and project out six to twelve weeks. Once you get the hang of this, you will find it easy to keep projecting out while updating the worksheet with actual data. Then next year, when you start planning, you can go back and get a weekly picture of your business operations.

Using a 52-Week Cash Flow is a practice that will help you to master your business through growth and downturns. Yes, even growth businesses require cash, and as you will see in the section on the sales trough, growth and working capital can consume cash faster than it can produce it, in the form of inventory, headcount or added support services putting you into a short-term cash crunch. Outgrowing your cash flow will land you in trouble just as fast as burning it on excessive expenses.

Why 52 weeks? This worksheet serves to plan future inflows and outflows of cash, and as you use it over the year, you will start to see monthly and quarterly trends that you can then incorporate into next year's budget.

The sheet is designed to automatically calculate key cash payments such as taxes and pay. In this example, we are simulating a husband-wife author team with multiple royalty streams and consulting fee streams that flow into a two-member LLC they have set up.

By tracking cash flow this way and projecting into the future incoming and outgoing cash, you will be able to do the following:

1. Identify cash flow issues before they happen. If you project you will run out of cash in ten weeks, there are things you can do today to eliminate the threat before it becomes a reality. This is your <u>#1 risk reduction tool.</u>

2. Become aware of the uses of cash. Some new business operators see a slug of cash come in and then spend it without understanding that a portion of that cash needed to be reserved for a future payment. Later, when the due date rolls up, they are short the cash and find they need to move money back in the business or get a loan.

On initial view, this worksheet may seem daunting. The concepts are simple.

Section One: Cash In

This section is where you put in each week's cash inflows. Create a line for each of revenue stream and put in the amount when you receive it in black or a projected payment in blue. The further you can project out, the better but also, the more accurately you can plan, the better.

In the example below, we show initial royalties from book sales in our cash in section. In the example projected, incoming cash is in blue text, and black text is used for actual collected payments. This begins a process of you developing the first part of the cash flow management knowing the source amount and time when cash should be coming in. In our example, the owner's main payments are coming from Apple and

Amazon, and they are specific dates that the payments come. With other types of customers, there may be credit extended on when they pay, and they may not always be timely. Seeing when the cash should be coming in and looking weekly will trigger you to check in for upcoming payments and adjust if there is a reason for payments slipping.

You can add more rows as needed.

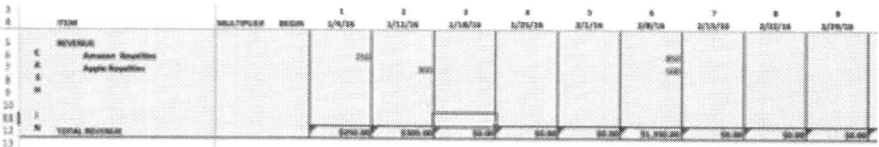

Section Two: Cash out

You will notice there are areas where the worksheet automatically calculates cash out around your pay and taxes. You will learn more about this in the expenses section and the philosophy of accruing cash to taxes and owner pay prior to expenses. The design of this form promotes your allocating funds in a way that keeps your taxes up to date and gets you paid something for your work.

The next section is cash out. For pay and taxes, there are percentage payouts that you set.

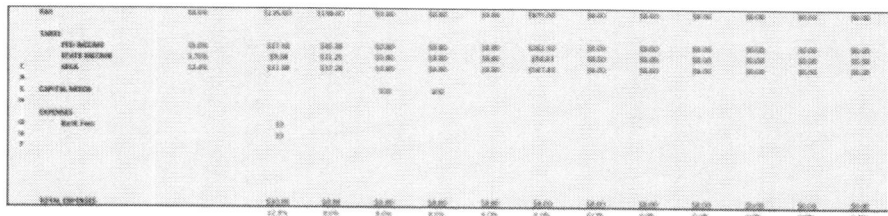

In the taxes section, you will see more information on determining your tax rate. Enter in applicable rates for taxes and pay—this is to assure that for all revenue that comes in, you allocate its portion to the owner pay and the associated tax liability. Remember that the tax allocation is not your money; you are holding it for the government.

With taxes and pay, the sheet calculates the amount you should allocate for each. I suggest that the tax portion be transferred out of your checking account into a savings account so you don't mistakenly use it for something else.

In the expenses section, track all the expenses related to your business. Just like with future projected payments, put in future projected expenses. Make sure that if your business is growing, you understand how that growth will impact future expenses.

Next is a capital allocation section where you can incrementally allocate capital to build up for an upcoming project. The capital accumulates in the third section. The last part of section two is the expenses section where you tally all your expenses and the specific week you pay them out.

Section Three is the cash management section where you can see the cumulative cash increasing and decreasing. The cumulative cash is the critical line to watch and go out as many weeks to the first negative number. Is it 13 plus weeks out? Good! Most likely, if you did further and better projections, this would go out further, but what if this is not the case or what if a negative number is sooner?

CASH		$142.13	$206.55	-$100.00	-$100.00	$0.00	$929.48	$0.00	$0.00
CUMULATIVE CASH	100	$242.13	$448.68	$348.68	$248.68	$248.68	$1,178.15	$1,178.15	$1,178.15
SAVINGS									
TAXES		$77.88	$93.45	$0.00	$0.00	$0.00	$420.53	$0.00	$0.00
TAX ACCT BALANCE		$77.88	$171.33	$171.33	$171.33	$171.33	$591.85	$591.85	$591.85
CAPITAL RESERVE		0	0	100	200	200	200	200	200
PAY									
TOTAL PAY									
TAXES				$0.00					
ACCOUNTS									
Checking 123	100	350	650	650	650	650	2000	2000	2000
Savings abc	500								
CHECK REGISTER									
Pay									
TRANSFER									

(CASH MANAGEMENT)

You need to address this immediately with action. Is this an expense issue? Is it a revenue issue?

The rest of the section is designed to help you actively manage your cash by accumulating your tax payments and showing distributions along with a section for a checking and savings account. This is an area for notation of checks you have cut, transfers made, and account balances. In a perfect world, this should balance with your checkbook and savings account. If you start doing this while you are small and have few transactions, you will get into the habit and keep the worksheet up to date.

My suggestion is that after you get familiar with the worksheet, you project out the next 12 months of your business on—this being the first attempt at getting a plan in place for your business. If you are a freelancer, contractor, self-published author, or digital seller, then starting with where your business is today and then projecting out where you want it to be will help you to formalize your thoughts and see what is most important to get to your goal. As you get used to the 52-week cash flow, you will see that you could run your operation off this sheet and your check book. And for just starting a smaller side business, this is a great start to being disciplined in your management of risk.

This is by no means the end all be all of cash flow management, but it has served me in the past to tracking cash and is a great start for someone new to these ideas and committed to learning how to manage cash.

As your business grows, you may need to plan for some capital expenditures like a new computer or new tools. The case may be that when you buy it, you will expense the item but consider setting up a capital reserve line on your cash flow to sock away funds so you can buy the item with cash rather than on a credit card. This practice will also help you to better grasp what cash you have for growing your business. This capital reserve line can be used to develop the working capital for future investment in your business (more on this in ROI)

About one to four hours a week is all you should need to update this sheet if you're in a single person self-employment situation.

Beyond the time, you spend updating the sheet when it's done, you need to look out to the next week and then through at least 13 weeks to be comfortable with your cash balance. As mentioned before, if you are using this tool right—and by that I mean you are updating into weekly reviewing the future projections of cash and then acting on the forecast now rather than when you're out of funds—you will be able to reduce the risk of running out of cash.

What to look for?

You should check the inflows first; keep an eye that receipts are increasing and being paid on time. If a customer is getting slow to pay, extending more credit won't get you paid faster and reduces your margins, as you are now banking customer business. If you see receipts slowing, make sure you adjust your expenditures in kind.

What to do if you see problems of negative cash flow developing? First look at cutting expenses and when planning cuts do 10% above what is needed.

After making sure you adjust your cash outflows, look to see what you can do to cause more sales.

I also include another cash flow sheet that I have used in the past for larger operations; this one covers 13 weeks. The layout of the worksheet is far less important than using the worksheet to run your business.

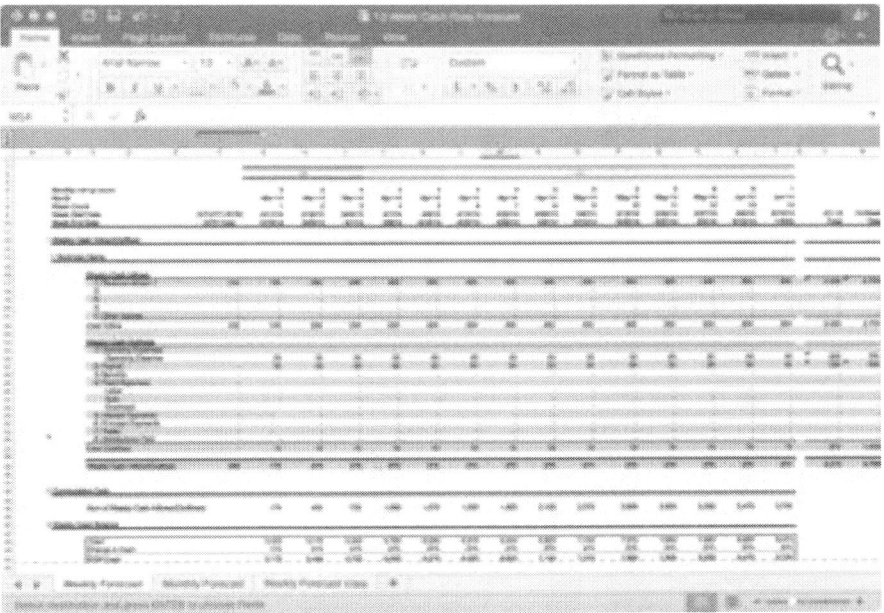

This one spreadsheet can do more for you to keep you out of financial trouble than any other statement or report, simply because you now have a window into the future of your business performance. In good times and bad, cash flow and the timing of when cash goes on and out of your business will have a serious effect. While most people think about a cash flow forecast to deal with disruptions to cash flow like a slow paying client, it is equally important in the planning of your cash needs for growth. As we will discuss in the sales trough and working capital, all business growth requires increases in capital, and sometimes these investments have a lag between the investment needed and the increased return of cash. If there is not cash allocated to cover this lag, you could slow or stop your growth because of the cash disruption.

PROFIT & LOSS THE INCOME STATEMENT

In the last section, we talked about cash flow and its importance. Now we will explore the income statement.

The purpose of the income statement is to show revenue, expenses, gains, and losses for a period. The period can vary. In most accounting packages, you can easily adjust the particular period you would like to report. The logical periods are monthly, quarterly, and annual.

Before we dive into the ins and outs of the income statement, let's first discuss the difference between cash and accrual.

Cash versus Accrual

If you run your business on a cash basis, you record sales when the cash hits the till (Bank Account) and record expenses when you pay them. For many businesses, this is a reasonable method of tracking your business, and when you do this, your Income Statement (or Profit and Loss) tells a pretty good story about where your cash is.

There are rules that require accrual accounting for certain size corporations, but most businesses under five million in revenue can use a cash basis.

When you are running an accrual based accounting process, then you show income when a sale is booked. This may be before you are paid, and you book expenses in association with the time or activity most relevant—even if you don't pay those bills until later.

When a sale is booked and no cash collected, it will be accounted for on the balance sheet as an account receivable, and expenses that you book but do not pay become an account payable. More on that in the balance sheet section.

This can present a false picture of solvency and intensifies the need for good cash flow management. Why? If you book a one-million-dollar sale but don't get paid, in accrual accounting, you have this big sale and potentially a big profit but no cash. You could owe taxes based on the profit but not have collected the cash you need to pay the taxes. Therefore, while accrual accounting does a good job associating the expenses with the revenues, it can present an unrealistic picture.

Think about it; if you book a bunch of sales and incur expenses to make those sales happen, those sales then must pay your suppliers before you get paid by the customer; you can run out of cash as outflows precede inflows.

Anyone who has found themselves in this situation knows the pain and suffering that is associated with cash flow dilemmas. If you are short of cash, and it is time to pay taxes or a payroll, you can quickly compound the problem with the additional expenses of fines for late taxes or the need to declare bankruptcy because you don't have the cash to keep pay past bills. If you have employees, nothing will kill moral faster than not making payroll. Keep in mind as you work with an income statement that it is not your cash flow; it is your paper profit and loss unless running a cash basis.

How do you know what way to run (cash Vs Accrual)? For smaller startups that are bootstrapping, cash is the way to go. Once you get over a half a million dollars, switching to Accrual starts to make sense. It is best to discuss with your tax preparer what they feel is a good cut over revenue number for the type of business you are running.

Following is a simple Income statement. While the subcategories can get detailed to help you to understand what impacts your profitability, all income statements have these common categories.

Sales	**100**
Cost of Goods Sold	60
Gross Profit	40
Expenses	10
Earnings Before Interest Taxes and Depreciation (EBITDA)	30
Interest	5
Depreciation	5
Operating Profit	20
Taxes (20%)	5
Net Profit After Tax (NOPAT)	**15**

Sales or Revenue:

Your top line is the gross sales you generate. You can further segment types of revenue to help you understand your income better.

Cost of Goods Sold (COGS):

This line is where you account for all the items and services directly associated with the product or service you sell. It will be subtracted from sales to get to your gross profit. You should include inventory used to fulfill the sale, freight, discounts, and any other direct costs for completing the sale.

Gross Margin:

This is the first margin line and shows you what you have left after you complete sales. Gross Margin is an indicator that you should track as a percentage of sales. In the case above, our GM is 40%; we keep an eye on this to make sure that fulfillment costs, freight, or inventory are not increasing and deteriorating our margins.

Expenses:

The costs associated with operating your business. They are payroll (but may not include owner's pay) utilities, cars, rent, etcetera. We will talk more about your expense levels later and how to control them, but at this point, expenses is the category where all non-COGS will be recorded except for Interest (if you have debt), Depreciation, and Taxes.

Earnings Before Interest Taxes & Depreciation(EBITDA):

When setting up your income statement, I suggest you have an EBITDA line so it is clear for you to view rather than traditional statements that require you to back Interest and Depreciation out of expenses to get EBITDA. EBITDA is a key indicator to value creation and provides an indication of the cash available for financing debt or flowing through to equity.

Earnings Before Interest Taxes, Depreciation, and Amortization is an important metric for your business and is THE GOLDEN STANDARD for business valuation. While there are dozens of methods to determine a business's valuation, it really boils down to EBITDA, as it provides a view of the business with the cost of debt service, non-cash expenses, and tax impact removed. Buyers find this information valuable because of the use of debt in a purchase transaction to improve the return on equity (more on this in valuation and other people's money) and need to be comfortable with the soundness of EBITDA to help them plan how they may structure debt as part of financing the purchase and future operations after purchase.

Interest:

If you have debt as part of your financing, this is a deductible expense; it needs to be subtracted from EBITDA to get to an operating profit.

Depreciation:

Depreciation is the current charge for asset use in that period. It is a non-cash charge and comes from a formula that figures the life of an asset and what portion should be charged for each particular period. It is important, as it is a non-cash deduction, meaning you paid cash in the past to buy an asset. As you use the asset each month or year, a portion is expensed on the income statement, like rent for use, but you spent no actual cash. This deduction reduces your tax liability.

Another consideration when thinking about depreciation is this: For most items that are depreciating; you have already made a significant cash outlay to procure the asset. That asset was purchased with after-tax dollars that could have been distributed to you as the owner. While in this period it was a cashless expense, cash was still used, and you are now "accounting for its use via wear and tear for the particular period.

Calculating Depreciation is complex and usually requires your accountant to develop depreciation tables. For many small businesses, capital purchases are so small that they just take the full expense in the current year and depreciation calculations are not required. If you do require them, many businesses do this at year end while tax preparation is done and then depreciation is expensed, and the assets is depreciated on the balance sheet.

Operating Profit:

The business profit prior to paying tax sometimes called pre-tax profit or operating profit. When setting up your chart of accounts, think carefully about how you want to use these terms. Depending on how you account for your interest and depreciation, operating profit and EBITDA could be the same in your accounts. This is the line that you figure your tax liability from at the end of the year. This is another line we should measure as a percentage of sales to keep an eye on.

Net Profit After Tax:

This is the actual profit or loss for the period after all revenues and expenses and payment of taxes.

Income statements typically show a period (monthly) data and sometimes also include year to date or comparison to a previous period to help you draw conclusions about your performance.

If you are a self-publisher or sell a product that provides a regular income like a royalty, then the IRS considers you self-employed, and this attracts the associated taxes with being self employed. This alone may push you into a more formalized accounting practice to help with your quarterly tax planning. This can be done with a simple cash-based income statement.

Expenses are a two-edged sword as a business owner. Every expense is our precious dollars out the door. Once spent on an expense, they are likely not coming back. On the other hand, as a business owner with a company charter, you can deduct all your expenses from your profits to determine a net profit that you pay taxes on. This opens the opportunity to have some expenses on your business that used to be after tax dollars become before tax expenses.

Don't fall for the illusion that this is free money. The actual money you are saving is the tax payment, not the expense. Here is an example:

Let's say you go to a conference, and it costs $560.00 for admission to the conference, travel to the conference, and meals. Your expense is $560.00.

Expensing the conference gives you a tax shelter of your tax rate times the expense. So, if your tax rate is 28%, you save $156.80 in taxes, but you out $403.20 in profit. Could that profit be used more wisely?

I bring this up because many new business owners fall into the trap of "perking up" the business. Now that they are the boss and there is no governing force, they start to run personal expenses "perks" through the business. This issue, being it is too much too soon, they find out later that the business can't support the costs. Let's look at some ways to evaluate expenses as you grow your business.

A good way to get a framework for any expense is to divide the expense by your gross margin to know what that expense equals in sales.

If I am spending $14 a month on a service and my gross margins are 30%, then each month, $46.66 of sales is needed to cover that expense. Now looking at the expense this way, I can evaluate the need versus the effort to get $46.66 in sales. This could be a very easy decision when the $14 spent makes it easy to get two or three times that in sales each month—Remember ROI.

Types of Expenses

Fixed

Fixed expenses are those that you have regardless of the amount of sales. Rent is a good example. Once you sign a lease for an office, you have the monthly expense the term of the lease, no matter what your level of sales. You need to really think through the addition to any fixed expense, especially payroll related ones, as they are either difficult or impossible to get rid of if your sales drop.

Variable Expenses are those that are tied to your revenue and go up and down with activity. While we want to make sure they stay in proportion to sales or reduce as sales scale up, the favorable feature is that they reduce or disappear as sales go down. By being proportional to sales, they are easier to deal with in a situation where sales drop.

Now let's take a more global view of expenses for the business. If you want to read a good book specifically on this topic, I suggest "Profit First" by Mike Michalowicz. It has a great approach to how to generate a profit, and it influences my recommendations as to how to think about budgeting in your business and scaling up in a way that generates the working capital your business will need.

You may be familiar with:

Revenue - Expenses = Profit

Standard fare if you are running a business and the core principles of accounting for a profit in your business. While this formula is true, you need to get a different mindset.

Revenue - taxes – paying you = what's left for expenses and Profits

Now don't look at this as advice to pay yourself before your vendors. What I suggest is, having a philosophy that as your business grows, you be deliberate and disciplined in how costs and your profit scale up in your business along with sales.

Many new business owners fall into the trap of letting expenses drive the business. No one is there to tell them how to plan or spend money. Having the flexibility to expense to the business items that, in the past, they could not or feeling as owners they should have certain fringe benefits, only later finding there is no profits or worse, no cash to pay themselves.

If your business is still in its formative stage, and it is hard for you to imagine being in a situation where you run a profitable business but, as the owner, you either don't get paid or end up putting in cash to cover taxes, beware it happens often. Another scenario is: Businesses have growth until there is some issue (loss of a customer, economic downturn), and the owner finds it seems impossible to cut expenses deep enough to get profitable. The best defense to this is to take a different approach as outlined here and scale profit and expenses to business growth. Always have a focus on the primary reason that you started your enterprise, achieving a certain lifestyle, and providing a return to you and other investors.

Now many owners believe part of being an owner is making sacrifices, but it doesn't have to be that everyone is profiting from your work but you. Your CEO title won't pay the rent. Instead, you need to start from day one carving out a percentage for you and keep this habit of aligning your compensation proportional to the revenues as the business scales up. This means sometimes something may need to be sacrificed, and I suggest it be adding additional expenses.

Doing this is fundamental to bootstrapping. If your only source of capital is that generated by the business, you must plan and allocate it appropriately. If buying a new vinyl printer is important for your sign business, then plan in the accumulation of equity to do this but also keep in mind there are a few other uses of cash that you need to set cash aside for at the same time. Evaluating any expense you plan to take on against its ability to grow the business is helpful.

Let's look at the example of a Vinyl printer. For a sign painter, the purchase of the printer is clearly going to help the business by reducing the cost of goods and increasing business capabilities. The $7,000 falls below a threshold where you could expense the printer rather than capitalize the equipment. The accounting treatment is not as important as understanding that the purchase of the printer takes $7,000 out of the company. Before purchase, analyze the impact:

A. Does the printer reduce the cost of goods across a range of work you know you have? If it improved cogs by 5%, do you have more than $145,000 worth of work in the next year or two? If so, then your return is going to be 50 to 100%. Good business choice!

B. Can you get new work because of the purchase? Will you get $23,000 of work at a 30% margin? Great! Buy the printer; it is 100% ROI.

Weighing all your expenses this way will help you to see those that can wait and those that are going to drive the business towards your goals.

To allocate for yourself, your taxes, and finally expenses, you will need to use some percentages to guide your business operations around three key areas:

- <u>Profit/Owner Pay</u>: **Allocate 30-50%.** Keep in mind corporate structure will influence this decision. If you are a sole proprietor or an LLC, you have a tax liability, including self-employment tax for <u>all profits</u> (Revenue-Expenses). If you are a C or an S corp, you should be on the company payroll, and your payroll tax is expensed. If you are running a corporation, then your payroll portion will be allocated to expenses, and you will need to allocate a portion of the owner pay and tax to expenses.

- <u>Taxes</u>: **Allocate 15-35%.** Your taxes are related to your entity structure. In the case of a Corporation, your payroll and payroll taxes will be expensed along with any other payroll, and therefore your tax allocation for profits will lower. If you have set up your business as an LLC, then you will be taxed on all profits along with a self-employment tax. The tax allocation is essentially just moving around and, generally speaking, taxes will take 15-35% when you tally up payroll or self-employment taxes along with income tax. The exact amount of taxes depends on the State of incorporation, while Federal taxes are applicable to all State business and income taxes are varied.

- <u>Expenses</u>: **Allocate 10-30%.** Before you decide to add expenses of any kind, either starting your business or growing it, you should always make sure you allocate the cash for taxes and for your hard work. After these two numbers are allocated, you can look at what there is for additional expenses.

If you explored the 52-week cash flow worksheet, then you may have noticed for pay and taxes, there were multipliers you could adjust to add tax and pay projections to your planning. The 52-week worksheet can act as your beginning business plan.

	AUTHOR	SMALL BUSINESS
REVENUE	$6,500	$120,000
Cost of Goods Sold COGS	$0	$78,000
Operating Profit	$6,500	$42,000
Taxes 35%	$2,275	$14,700
Post Tax	$4,225	$27,300
Owner Pay	$3,250	$13,650
Money for Expenses	$975	$13,650

Look at the table below that has two examples. One is a self-publishing author that is just getting started with some sales and beginning to plan when they may go to full-time writing; the other is a small online sales business that is buying products overseas and selling through E-

Retailers with an outsourced fulfillment model. In both cases, when we are looking at percentages, they need to be worked off your gross profit dollars, not revenue, unless you have no cost of goods.

Let's discuss the author first, as he is planning to someday work from home but knows that it is not a reality to quit the day job just yet. He has estimated that year one sales for his first book will be $6,500. He has no costs to produce his sales, as he self-publishes and has all the sales reporting and accounting done by the E-book retailer. He gets paid monthly on the previous month's sales. We will discuss figuring your tax liability in the tax section but for ease of example, let's agree that Federal and State income tax, including self-employment, runs 35%. We estimate $2,275 for annual taxes; that money needs to be sequestered in a savings account and not touched except to make quarterly tax estimate payments. If he does not do this, he will get a surprise at end of the year when the expected tax refund turns into a tax and penalty payment because he was short $2,275 on 6,500 in income.

Next is owner pay. Too many owners get themselves in a place where they are no longer the master but the servant of the business. They have added expenses or employees, and by the time they pay them plus taxes, they find there is nothing for them. Or worse, they must put additional capital to grow the business or cover cash flow gaps. So, if you only follow one thing in this book, this is the section because it will do more to keep you in control of your business.

Your Compensation needs to be next about.

Here are some rules of thumb:

Work to capture 50% of the post-tax cash in your pocket. In the beginning, this may seem silly that you're writing a $75 check to yourself, but it builds the habit and discipline that will get you to do the same when it is the amount that lets you quit your day job. Enjoy the process of growing your business from maybe paying a bill or two to covering your next Holiday to one day giving you the freedom to quit your day job.

Later, that 50% may be far more than what others in a similar role would get paid, so you may adjust the percentage down, but you should be overpaid; you put in the hard work, and if you are equally disciplined in keeping expenses in line, you most likely had to do a lot of extra work early on to conserve.

Expenses

So, our estimate shows that our Author has the guide of $975 cash available for expenses for day-to-day operations or future capital expenditure. This kind of money could go to cover the initial formation of an LLC or Corporation or get a nice website with some marketing going. Maybe it goes to getting cover art done for book two or hiring an editor. The choice is hers if she respects the $975 limit.

The Small Business

For the example of the small business, there is a 65% cost of goods that includes buying the inventory, fulfillment costs, and freight.

For those that are classically trained in business, the income statement is the driving report for of business performance, and the convention of Sales – Expenses = Profit/Loss will be tough to break from.

This is a budgeting exercise and requires you to be proactive in applying the limits on the business. If you are not someone that is going to go too deep into financials, then you should be comfortable with using these guidelines to help you with your decision-making process and in the case of our small business example, if you were the owner, you would need to keep expenses in line with the $13,650. You will find if you adopt this process and discipline, you let expenses get out of control, and you will have money you could allocate for additional expenses, but it literally comes out of your pocket since the owner's allocation would need to be reduced.

What if I find that my Expenses are too high?

You may be reading this book and faced with a drop-in sales or other unfortunate bumps in the road that leave you facing high expenses and struggling with cash flow.

I suggest you look at your business a different way; understand your gross profit is what is left after the goods are bought and sold, inclusive of freight and handling/installation costs. This Gross profit is the key number to work from. From your gross profit, next, determine what you expect to make and want to deliver as a profit (10%).

What is left is what is available to cover expenses; compare that to what you are currently paying in expenses and subtract the difference from that extra amount:

Current expenses - estimated expenses = difference X 1.1 = what you need to cut

This will be a painful exercise, but after completing the process, you will now have the respect to not let expenses get out of control and will use the formula to guide your business budget.

If the case is you are running a small cottage business that you are looking to take to the next level, this is a great exercise to go through and see where the conflict lies. You may find yourself saying:

"Hey, I have not taken a salary because the business expenses are too high and that's why I need to grow the business."

If this is your thinking, then ask this question: "Why will expenses not increase in proportion to sales?" In most cases, poor discipline is the cause of expenses getting out of control. Get them down so that you can pay yourself something, and from that day forward, reward you for your work.

Gross Margin − (Salary + Profit + Taxes) = cash for expenses. This is your budget!

If the case is you plan to bootstrap (more on this later), then this practice will be critical for methodical scaling up of the operation and producing the necessary working capital organically.

WHAT IS A BALANCE SHEET?

The balance sheet is a snapshot at a point in time of the business assets and liabilities. An important but sometimes confusing tool used to evaluate the general health and durability of the business.

Remember that the Cash Flow, Income Statement, and Balance Sheet are all tied to each other and changes to one impact the other two. While many owners look to the income statement for business performance, your creditors and buyers of the business will look to the balance sheet to see if the business is creditworthy, by showing that there is a surplus of equity and assets to offset any current liabilities or future ones you may be taking on such as debt.

There also is an overarching formula that is the basis of the balance sheet:

Assets = Equity + Liabilities

The balance sheet needs this equation to balance, and when it doesn't, it is a sign of poor accounting or something in the underlying business not adding up.

The balance sheet is also where you will see value accumulate in the form of Equity.

Here are the different sections of the balance sheet and what they represent:

Assets:

These are the items of value that the business possesses and include things like, cash, buildings, land, cars, accounts receivable

Cash

This is the funds you have in your checking and savings account, as well as other liquid financial instruments.

Accounts Receivable

This is how we deal with selling to a customer on an accrual basis but not getting paid until a later period. We book the sale on the balance sheet and note the sale as an account we will receive in the future. This is considered an asset with the assumption that the customer will pay his account within terms and the account receivable will become cash (an asset) soon. Accounts receivable can be used as collateral for loans.

Property, Plant & Equipment

Some businesses buy assets like a building, car, or computer equipment. Those assets have value and, depending on the type of asset and its value, you may end up including them on your balance sheet along with tracking the depreciation of the asset. How different assets are treated needs to be discussed with your tax preparer. Sometimes the decision will be to expense the asset in that year and then not have to do any depreciation calculations; other times, you will have to create a depreciation schedule. Since there are IRS rules for depreciation and they change from time to time, this need be part of your conversation about taxes.

Liabilities: These are obligations of the business to others. Anyone that looks to loan money to the business as debt will be interested in the ratio of liabilities to equity and look to make sure that the assets of the business can cover any outstanding debt. You will learn more about ratios in the Ratios you should know section.

Loans: Long and short term debt taken on by the business. Long-term debt obligations are those over one year in duration; conversely, short term is less than one year.

Accounts Payable: These are obligations from trade credit to your vendors. The account is associated with expenses you accrue on your income statement but have yet to pay in the same period.

Equity: This is a source of assets and a claim on those assets by the owners of the equity. Your initial contributions of cash to start the business creates equity in the business; any additional contributions also increase the equity in the business. The other way equity is created is from retained earnings that the enterprise has generated.

There can be different classes of equity in a business. For small, simple businesses, there is usually just one, but if you do raise money from outside investors, they may have obligations pertaining to the preference of the equity or how dividends are paid.

I won't belabor the balance sheet. It is a critical piece of accounting, and you should eventually get to know your way around it. In most small businesses, your tax preparer can put one together off your Income statement as part of your tax return at year end. If you don't have reporting requirements for creditors, an annual balance sheet will suffice and is required as part of completing your tax returns for your business.

If your operation is larger, and you are using an accounting package, then the Balance Sheet is core to double entry accounting, and you can print out the report on a regular basis.

WORKING CAPITAL

What is working capital and why do you need to worry about it?

The definition of Working Capital is the capital of a business that is used in its day-to-day trading operations, calculated by subtracting current liabilities from current assets. In other words, if you took all your current debts and bills and subtracted them from the cash and incoming cash that is due (receivables), that amount that is left over is the cash you must operate the business.

Your business starts to have operational issues when the amount of working capital on hand is less than the working capital the business requires.

Symptoms of working capital issues:

- You need to extend creditors out past agreed terms, or these vendors are placing your account on hold
- You are concerned about meeting financial obligations like payroll

Main reasons for working capital issues

- Continued losses
- Growth outpacing the cash collection cycle

Working capital is tied closely to cash flow but is different. A positive cash flow is the ability of a business to produce working capital organically. Working capital is the pool of cash you have available and is sometimes referred to as your company's liquidity. If cash is the oxygen of the business, then working capital is a measurement and understanding of the lung capacity of your business. If the cash is not there to support the business, then it will begin to perform inefficiently and eventually stop working at all.

What you need to keep in mind with working capital is that as your business grows, so will the pool of cash that needs to be in the business to keep things moving smoothly. When looking at a balance sheet, you will find your working capital residing in cash on hand, accounts receivable, and Inventory.

A growing business will require more working capital, regardless if you sell a product or a service. In the case of a product-based business, cash is needed to keep the level of service you want for your clients by adding inventory. If your inventory turnover is constant, then for each new customer, your inventory will increase by approximately the average customer sales for the given inventory turnover period.

For example, if you turn over inventory every two months and your average monthly sales are $1,200 with average margins of 30%, then your inventory will increase by $1,680 for each customer, or you will begin to have stock outs. If you also extend credit to a new customer, then, along with the inventory needs, your cash collection cycle will also grow in volume, thereby increasing working capital needs.

$1,200 a month sales

30% Gross Margin = Cogs of $840

Inventory turnover = 6 times a year = need $1,680 in inventory added for each customer (this could increase initially if you have a sourcing lag on new orders)

Each customer gets 30 days' credit = 30-day lag on cash collection

If you must pay your supplier in 30 days, then your new customer just cost you $1,680 prior to getting in dollar one.

Service businesses are no different and sometimes suffer more, as those providing the service look to be paid in a shorter time than clients typically pay. You will suffer the same fate as a product based business, as you will need to add service providers to support the new clients. In fact, some service businesses feel a further squeeze because they must outsource higher cost contract service while finding good internal service providers.

See the sales trough section to learn more about planning for growth and how to visualize the length and depth of the hole a growth initiative can create.

Isn't high growth rate good, no matter what it is? Not when it absorbs all your cash, creating cash flow issues. So be careful! Even when you're profitable and growing, know what each new customer requires in cash to get through onboarding. If you're not sure, then work through the sales trough section.

All businesses will see working capital shrink when they suffer losses. The mechanics are that the costs of operations exceed the profits and those expenses are paid with cash that won't be around to be used in future working capital cycles. Your lung capacity is the same but next time you breathe, there will be less oxygen to breathe in. Sometimes called a burn rate. If you are not profitable, you should have a deep understanding of how much cash you burn a week and the number of weeks you must get to your break-even point.

Working Capital Management

You can manage your working capital accumulation, and with your 52-week cash flow, you will be able to see the impact of your business operations on your cumulative cash balance.

If part of your business plan is to increase sales, you can always test your assumptions using the 52-week cash flow as a planning tool. You can do this by projecting out sales on a copy of the 52-week CF. Here's how:

Make a copy of your 52-week worksheet, then project out your sales growth building in your customer growth, <u>apply your average collection days</u> so that you have the appropriate lag in cash collection with the new sales growth. This will model the cash flow lag.

If you will be hiring more sales people or your new initiative uses a commissioned based sales channel, build in those costs into the cash flow. You may also need to add other staff or support costs; make sure those are included in your expenses. Don't forget any one-time costs such as installation costs or recruiting costs. Next, build in inventory build and the payments for those goods.

Now look at this cash flow model and see if you see cash deficits develop. This is where you need to evaluate how you're going to turn down the growth or the expenses you plan for this initiative to get the process cash flow positive.

Inventory

If your business is growing at a rate of 10% per year, over that year, you will need to increase your inventory levels year over year, and more of your assets will get absorbed into the operations.

$10,000; by year end, this will be $11,000. Now that is not a big move figuring about $84 a month in additional cash required to keep the right inventory levels. Now that cash will not be available for other needs like paying taxes or your pay and is stranded in the business as inventory until you reduce inventory levels. In operations, we go into <u>inventory</u> optimization and in doing this, you can improve turn and get your inventory to have a higher liquidity. Inventory is the trickiest part of working capital because it is not as liquid as cash. Cash can be deployed to other areas of your business as needed but once cash is converted to inventory, then you need to go through the sales cycle to convert it back to cash. Having your cash sitting in inventory can really be painful. There are ways to limit your inventory needs while growing. The best is if you can come to an agreement with your vendors for extended terms or consignment inventory. This is vendor financing of your growth and provides you additional working capital.

Growth

Anytime your business grows, it will use and hold capital. There tends to be an up-front capital loading to initiate the growth. Then as growth continues the business will establish a new minimum working capital level that must be sustained for smooth operations. Understanding the balance between your growth rate and your available working capital is the secret to continued sustained growth without the need for outside capital. By testing your plans and determining if you will run out of cash, you can either back off on your growth plan, or you can defer the initiative and build up a cash reserve to support the plan.

Rainy Day

When fortune or misfortune comes, are you prepared to act—and by prepared, are you ready with cash? Bad circumstances can become worse if you are unable to have the cash to get through a downturn. Conversely, you may miss out on opportunities because you are unable to take advantage of the situation with the ability to write a check. Your first goal with working capital is to work to have a one-month operating cash on hand and then work this to one-quarter. This will go a long way to ending sleepless nights, knowing you have the runway to work with.

Managing Working Capital Takeaways

1. Work to develop your general working capital fund

Goal 1 One Month of Operation

Goal 2 One-Quarter of Operation

2. Monitor business changes to adjust your needs

3. Plan growth projects and test your working capital balance by using the 52-week cash flow worksheet

4. If you find your capital will be an issue, set up a line to allocate cash in reserve for future growth.

BUDGETING

Budgets live in that interesting place between planning and finances. Yes, a budget is a planning tool but your budget bridges over to operations and finance when used properly. It should be more than just an exercise that you complete once which then it goes in a drawer. It is your numerical guide to measure progress towards your goal, the ruler to validate you as to how reality is in comparison to your plan.

When a budgeting process is done completely, you have cash flow, income statement, and the beginning and ending balance sheet for a specific period of time that represents your best estimates for what success looks like. Going through this process gives you confidence that you have thought through all the possibilities and tested assumptions. Later in financial modeling, I will introduce you to some dynamic modeling tools that are fantastic for planning and projecting results when you are faced with variability and uncertainty, but for most entrepreneurs, they will get the most bang for their buck by creating a basic budget and then reviewing it monthly against actual results.

Why?

The budget gives you a frame of reference to a plan that you believe will deliver your estimated results in the future. Once completed start executing that plan, revisit the budget when you need to be reminded of what the plan was, and what progress looked like. Without that reminder, the day-to-day dilemmas and agendas of others will pull you away from your intention, and you will find yourself chasing butterflies rather than moving deliberately towards your goal.

If you have partners or plan to raise outside funds, then you will need to have done some deep budgeting and planning work. You need to do this so you can confidently speak to the plan and sell the deal to investors. Any serious investor will want to see a solid budget with three to five years of projections to see how serious you are about the project and to have material to test your assumptions. Without that level of planning, there is really nothing you must offer other than a story about your dream.

The Beginner Soloprenuer Budget

If you are on your own and are a little intimidated with all the financial statements but want to step up your game, I suggest a slightly different approach.

You start by making a simple budget. This can be on a scratch pad, or you can use the template provided on the website. Start by capturing the main points of your current state and where you want to be in twelve months.

Revenue: Current run rate and future goal.

You should also make some notes about your thoughts on how revenues scale between the two points.

Expenses: Current expenses, expenses you think you will need to add to scale up, and the expenses that you will have when you meet plan.

Keep in mind the types of expenses (fixed and variable) and how they will be needed to achieve your plan. Categorize the types and estimate the ratio of expense to revenue for those that are variable.

Profit/Loss: This is essentially going to be math. You don't necessarily need to figure this out before the next step because if you use the 52-week sheet, it will get you there.

Funding: If you have a feel for your needs, great! But the next step will show you your needs clearly. If your plan produces a negative cash balance in the cumulative cash section, you will need a source of funds to get through the plan.

Next build—make a copy the 52-week cash flow and using the simple budget you just made, plug numbers into the various points. I suggest taking a monthly approach and building the costs as best as you can plan into each month, but you could also just use the first 12 weeks to represent each month. You will find that by using the full 52-week cash flow and building it out as a one-page working budget, later, you can use another copy as your actual working cash flow and have an easy comparison tool.

Let me make a point here: if you were to do just as I described, you would be setting yourself up to be a top performer, putting yourself in the small percentage of companies that budget; more important is your using this in conjunction with your weekly planning and review will keep you later focused and out of trouble.

With a new business, you are working from more of your vision than actual data; this process helps you to see the vision coalesce and become a reality.

If you have been operating your business by the seat of your pants, then implementing this process with the 52-week cash flow/budget will get you a picture of your current state. Then use that baseline and give you clarity on where to put your efforts to get the business on a plan, scaling your business in alignment with your purpose. Without taking the time to plan to that purpose, how can it ever be?

Budgeting: Setting a plan and then systematically evaluating each period of your performance to the plan and acting to keep in accordance with the budget.

Why do I need a budget if I am using the fifty-two-week cash flow?

If all you get from this book is the habit of using cash flow analysis to project out your positive or negative cash flow, then you will have established a habit that will serve your whole life and contribute to your ongoing success. You will succeed because, unlike 95% of small business owners, you have foresight into cash flow upsets that will catch all the others off guard.

When you add budgeting to the process, your ability to evaluate your current circumstances increases. Budgeting is not about setting a plan and rigidly following that plan; it is about having INTENTION towards a goal and writing your best guess as to how to make the intention real. As time passes, you get data to compare to the budget and then through analysis, you decide, *Am I doing what I planned? Am I getting better or worse results and what can I do to get back on plan or do better?*

Maybe some phenomenal opportunity comes along that you need to act on; you can change the plan, but when you do so, you are coming from a place of knowledge and have a context to evaluate any new opportunities.

ANNUAL BUDGET PROCESS

At what point should you do a formal annual budgeting process?

I believe the benefit that an annual budget process has for getting you strategic is invaluable. If you are running an operation and are comfortable with income statements and balance sheet but don't use them in a formal budget process, then creating a monthly budget income statement and cash flow will help you to think through how your vision can be converted into wealth and, most importantly, understanding the costs and tradeoffs that come with the plan. Specifically, the budget works hand-in-hand with your business plan to set a numerical model of your expected outcome and gives you a place to start to figure out what might be going wrong.

Let's say you see cash flow generation at a slower pace than you expected. You can now quickly compare the last few month's income statements against the budget and get an anchor to what is out of line

Revenue: Is it lower? Then you're missing your sales projection and can begin to evaluate how to impact the top line.

Gross Margin: Is it lower? Then your cost of goods has increased. Now we can focus our effort on those costs and get back on budget

Operating Income: Have some expenses gotten out of line and taken away from your projected income? Even if you don't have a line item budget, you know to consider expenses and where there is a variance.

The uncertainty and wondering go away when you know where to look and have a general idea of what the contributing factor might be.

The essence of the budget tool is this:

1. If you look at them regularly, you see problems sooner.

2. It expedites a solution because you spend less time looking for the cause.

You can use our budgeting worksheet or use the planning worksheet that your tax preparer uses to build out a monthly budget that totals for the year.

Some accounting software programs will develop budgeting from historical information or allow to enter a budget into the system. Before diving in, understand what doing that work will offer you. My experience is, it is easier to lay a profit and loss next to a budget and compare them on paper than going through hours of setting up budgets in a software. If I do need to integrate them, I typically export actuals to an excel file from the accounting package and then merge it into the budget to make side-by-side comparisons.

If you are already overwhelmed, you may think that you don't have time to plan or to follow up by checking a budget. You are going to need to trust me on this process that by using a budget, you will be able to get a better grasp on your business operations. You should allocate strategic time each month to do the work of updating your financials or reviewing them if someone else is doing the bookkeeping. Be proactive, not reactive!

The important work of budgeting is not how much you invest in making the reports but how you use them to evaluate your performance.

First, get the ratios of owner pay and expenses right, and then review and adjust when you see problems. If you have adopted the 52-week cash flow, then, in some respects, your budget and other financials become second fiddle. You go to them when you see issues developing with cash and use the tools to determine where margins or expenses may be moving away from your plan and budget.

For the self-employed, your budget is also a way to see that you're on track for the growth you set out to achieve. Use this tool to check in monthly and quarterly for progress and how you may need to adjust to keep momentum.

Process for creating a 12-month Budget when you have prior year financials

Get last year's income statement to build this year's budget from. If you don't have them, you will be developing estimates and projections.

Input them into the worksheet; look to place expenditures in the appropriate month where they fall so that you will have your budget representative of what happens. There is a big difference to your cash flow if an annual expense is spread out evenly over twelve months or it occurs once a year.

Establish key performance results (KPRs) for your budget. Typically, there is emphasis on

gross margin percentage expenses as a percentage of sales.

You may set out during this process areas that require longer term strategic work to improve. Here is when and where you set those goals; later is when you make sure your tactics are driving you towards your strategy goal.

Review your budgets monthly as part of your monthly financial analysis. Start by making sure the big number of revenue, gross margin, and operating income are in line; if not, home in to find the culprit.

During your Monthly Review:

If you see a category that is off by 5% or more, highlight it; determine why.

If you have a category that is off by 10% or more or if it has been off two or more months, do a deep dive to determine the issues.

The budget provides the warning lights that means 'it's time to do some maintenance.' You can keep driving but don't be surprised when the engine locks up if you never do the tune up.

A Budget for Leaving Your Day Job

Another type of budget is one that plans the achievement of your goal of self-employment within a fixed period. Your conviction to become your own boss through self-employment will happen faster if you have a plan and understand what it will require in time, effort, and capital to leave your day job.

Begin with the plan for your business. Going through this process will help you to understand better the costs associated with running your own business and determine when you will have the savings and revenues built up to exit your day job.

If you have planned, and you understand what you will need to leave your day job, remember: with plans, they never work out as envisioned, but if you have the determination and energy, the result will be better than what your initial plan envisioned.

Plan to raise money?

I have sat in on several investment pitches as well as done a few myself. As someone who has seen many people present generic financial plans or very flimsy ones, I'll let you in on what goes through the heads of the decision maker. It falls somewhere between being uninspired to disbelief but no matter where the financial presentation falls on that spectrum, they politely smile and take a pass. There are three criteria:

1. The investment must be realistic and compelling.

2. The financial model needs to be solid and well thought out.

3. The person that will make the plan become a reality needs to have intimate knowledge and command of the model.

If all the three are in place, that gets you to a point where the potential investor will take your numbers and really dig into your numbers, and as they do, they will likely discount your projections to determine what they believe the return profile really is.

The point is, if you are serious about raising money for your venture, even if you are looking at doing a pitch at an event and only have five minutes, you need to be one with your financial projections.

The traditional business school methodology is to present a low, middle, and optimistic projection to give your investors a better feel for where the opportunity may end up. The time frame is typically five years. The reasoning on the timeframe is, most private equity firms have an investment horizon of five years. You project out your business plan into the future for five years of growth, and then apply a low and high projection off your normal view.

If you remember our discussions of risk and growth, we covered that while GDP may have an average growth of 3.5%, the range of variance is -9.5% to 16.5%, so I think these models that project steady growth rates with little variance are suspect. If you are serious about estimating risk and doing a complex model of potential outcomes, I suggest you look at some examples of dynamic modeling that use Monte Carlo simulations to create thousands of random possibilities and then use statistics to apply probabilities to the outcomes.

Think about how different your presentation would be if you said to investors, "Rather than giving you three guesses at how the business may turn out, I have built my model so that I did 50,000 iterations with all the variation of the real world and based on those probabilities, this is what I see is the probability of success and the return on investment you seek."

Chances are you are going to be taken more seriously, and they will infer that you will bring the same diligence to the operation of the business if you are funded.

The next chapter dives deeper into funding your venture.

FINANCING YOUR BUSINESS

IN THIS CHAPTER, I will cover how Capital is used in your business. The various ways small business owners source capital, the cost of capital to your business, and then get into the specifics of debt and equity. Finally, I will cover how most small businesses are financed and discuss ways to finance your business venture, beginning with start-up financing, and then exploring ongoing growth and working capital sourcing, including new sources like crowdfunding.

Let's begin by introducing another term.

Capital Stack: The layers of capital used to finance a business and the relationship they must have with each other.

Sometimes these layers of capital are called tranches.

The basic tranches in any business are Debt and Equity. Then within equity and debt, there can be further layers, each with features of priority and return.

Within the stack, there is priority—meaning the claims that the different forms of finance have on the assets of the business. Remember the balance sheet; the top half is the assets of the business, cash, accounts receivable, inventory, and property. The lower half is the liabilities and equity. So when we talk of priority of claims, it is the rights for the funding at the bottom half of the balance sheet on the assets on the top.

Debt has priority over equity on the claims to business assets. If you were liquidating a business, you would sell all the assets, collect all the cash—and the first to receive that cash would be the debt providers. Then the money left over would go to the equity holders.

With debt and equity, there can be further prioritization. The first example is the company has decided to liquidate and has $45,000 in cash to satisfy a bank loan of $25,000 and $15,000 of vendors that have extended credit. After paying all the creditors in order of priority, the common stockholders only get $5,000. If the amount of cash were $30,000, then the business, being insolvent, would pay the full amount of the secured loan, and then distribute the remaining funds to the unsecured creditors, with the common shareholders getting nothing.

Example #1

Debt

Total value of assets $45,000

$25,000 in secured loans

$15,000 unsecured creditors

Common Stockholders get $5,000

There can be further prioritization with types of equity. Such as Preferred Equity that a part of the terms of its issuance is that it gets paid first prior to common equity. In example two, we add another layer of $3,000 of equity that has the conditions of a 5% dividend and up to 1.2 times payment in a liquidation or sale prior to common stock getting paid.

Example #2

Debt

Total value of assets $45,000

$25,000 in secured loans

$15,000 unsecured creditors

Preferred Equity gets $3,600

Common Stock holders gets $1,400

When visualizing your capital stack, see it as a series of funding layers, each with different terms, different return rates, and different priority as to claims on the company assets.

This leads to another concept you should understand: **Cost of capital**

Cost of capital is an important metric to understand about servicing the sources of finance. Your cost of capital is the capital providers expected return on investment. If your bank loan is at 12%, the bank is looking for an ROI around 12%. Just like outside investors, your investment requires a return, and when you take all of the different sources of capital and blend them together, you get the WACC or Weighted Average Cost of Capital, the return your business needs to provide to deliver the results expected by all of the investors, including you.

Once you know your cost of capital, you should evaluate every investment against it. If your cost of capital is 10%, then if you run an ad campaign for $100, it should return at least $110 in profit, not sales (more on this in evaluating investments).

So how do you figure out your cost of capital?

Your cost of capital is the blended rates of the debt and equity returns used to finance your business. The rate blend is weighted according to the amount of each type of capital.

Earlier, I suggested an equity hurdle of 14% for your business. That was determined by doubling the S&P500 average return. This is just a rule of thumb, not an actual cost of capital. You may have a different cost of equity negotiated for the equity in your business based on the suppliers of the equity, but if your cash is the source of equity, your investor alter ego needs his return, and it needs to be better than just putting into an index fund, hence 14%. Now we will discuss what "your cash" is really costing you if you are providing debt via a credit card you personally guarantee.

In an example where the only source of finance was your savings that was put into the company as equity, your cost of capital is easy 14%.

But what if you are like most entrepreneurs that you personally secured debt to fund the business start-up, and like the majority, you leverage debt to equity by two to five times the amount of equity?

In the example above, let's keep the numbers round and say that you start the business with $1,000 in cash from your savings and then use credit card debt on a card that has a 16% interest rate for another $2,000 for a total equity of $3,000.

Total Capital = $3,000

Equity = $1000 X 14% = $140

Debt is a little more complex since interest rate is tax deductible, so we have this formula that includes the tax rate influence on interest. For our example, we will use 35%:

Debt = (1- tax rate) X 16% X $2,000

Debt = (1-.35) X 16% X $2,000 = .65 X 16% X $2,000 = $208

We now add the two weighted averages $140 + $208 = $348

Finally, divide the sum by the total capital $348 / $3,000 = 11.6%

Now if you are shaking your head as to how this ended up being lower, it is because debt has the advantage that the interest is a tax-deductible expense and is modified by your tax rate and is further compounded by the two-to-one weighting.

Let's do another example with the scenario being you have a personal line of credit with the local bank or a home equity line that you can draw on. Again, you have an initial equity stake of $1,000 from your savings and $4,000 from your home equity line for a total capital stack of $5,000. The rate on your home equity line is 6.5%:

Equity = $1,000 X 14% = $140

Debt = $4,000 X 6.5% X (1-35%) = $169

$140 + $169 / 5,000 = 6.18%

You can begin to see how the use of lower cost debt (sometimes lower because of the tax shield) can reduce your cost of capital and help you to boost your returns on equity because every one of your higher cost equity dollars has one or more lower cost debt dollars working with it. This is known as leverage, and it is the most powerful tools private equity uses to boost returns and a good lesson for you to use an appropriate amount of low-cost debt to fuel your business growth.

The tradeoff is that the debt provider has a higher claim on the assets of the business than you do as the owner.

Popular belief is that small businesses are typically funded from one of these three sources: Owner's Equity, Friends and Family, or Venture Capital. The other common concept of capital structure is the concept of the pecking order that an owner will start first with his own equity, then go to the next expensive form of capital, being outside debt, and then go to the most expensive capital, being outside capital. Both concepts are flawed.

The research I use for this section draws on the data from the Kauffman Foundation surveys on firms and supplementary surveys about capital structure decisions that these same firms have made. The basis of the survey is the ongoing work the Foundation has done tracking 4,928 firms from 2004 through the current data in 2011 (published in 2013).

The survey population is relevant in my opinion because 59.2% of the firms had no employees in 2004 survey, and of those firms surviving in the 2011 (44.6% survival), survey data shows that 47.4% had no employees, giving us a population that is skewed to the solo operator and small business. Of firms that did have employees, the majority had 1–9 employees, with only 9.5% having ten or more, so this is good data for assessing the microcap segment of businesses.

What the Kauffman data shows is that debt plays a significant role in small business in the form of debt held by the owner or the business with guarantees by the owner.

Simply put: single employee businesses have high leverage because the owner's equity is personally guaranteed credit card debt.

Why is this important?

If you are like most small business owners and you source financing in the same way, then the cost associated with these sources of finance will be similar. You won't be tapping into private equity capital or traditional bank debt until your business has established a history of profitable operation.

Therefore, the best way to gain access to a larger pool and lower cost capital is to demonstrate your understanding and return on the capital you currently use.

There is also a cost of time in sourcing capital. Time is, by far, your most precious resource and once you look to source outside capital, the process can consume 50% or more of your time to source expensive capital.

Prior to embarking on a quest for new capital, you need to understand the uses of the capital and the expected results. Even in a situation where an equity provider is prepared to invest in a plan where there is a period where there is a negative cash flow, they want to see a realistic plan to profitability and continued growth. Equity providers will take that risk to get early access to high growth that will, in turn, become a return on equity; debt providers will not.

The most common solution for startup capital is your saving and a combination of using credit cards or personal debt (like a home equity loan) to initially fund your business and then bootstrap your business.

As your business grows and builds creditworthiness, you can improve the cost of this capital by exchanging more expensive sources of capital for lower ones particularly in debt. The facts of life are that banks and other lenders will say they are there to support you and your dream, but they are in the business of getting a risk-adjusted return for their investors. The investor is the customer you are not.

All this means your best approach to business funding is to be realistic about the answers to the following question:

Do you have 2-3 years of profitable operation?

Do you have a realistic plan for the use of funds?

Do you have Good Credit?

Are you prepared to provide a personal guarantee for the debt?

Have you done adequate planning and modeling to be confident that your use of the additional funds will result in your plan?

Many will find that with honest answers to the questions, the best approach is to revise the plans for the business and get growth in alignment with the capital you can source with the lowest WACC and time cost.

The Capitalization Table

A capitalization table is a document that lists the various types of capitalization or layers and the owners of those layers with corresponding percentages of ownership.

If you have outside investors, a cap table is a mandatory document to track the claims all investors have on assets. This document is also used each year for tax preparation if you have a "pass through" entity to allocate profits and losses to the investors.

EQUITY

Equity is a source of assets and a claim on those assets.

Equity comes into the business usually as capital paid in for ownership. The business also can generate equity through the generation of profits and retaining those earnings into the business. The equity created via retained earnings increases the overall value of the company and each owner's stake proportionally.

When setting up your business, you will have formation capital; typically, this is the funds to incorporation and some seed capital. If you're a solo operator, the capitalization (Cap Table) is simple; you have 100% of the equity. If you have partners or a variety of equity types, then the capitalization and claims on assets will be different

Types of equity

Shares and Units

When you incorporate, the type of company you set up will determine if the company has shares or units. If you incorporate, you will have shares, and each share of a class has the exact same value and voting rights.

If you chartered an LLC, then each member of the LLC has a capital account. You may remember from the chapter should I incorporate the rights of the LLC members are stipulated in the operating agreement. Many times, when outside investment is sought, equity is sold as units of membership in an LLC and those units could also have various classes. The rights and features of those classes would be designated in the LLC operating agreement.

Just as there are different types of debt, there are also different categories of equity. Below are a list and description of the commonly used forms of equity. Other than common shares, the types of equity apply to both LLCs and corporations.

Forms of equity

Common shares

Common shares are the form of equity that most corporations use. Each share has a specific value, and it is equal to all other shares in that class and has one vote. In some companies like Viacom and Facebook, there are different classes of shares. In the case of the two companies noted, one share has voting rights associated with it and no dividend; any other share class has no voting rights but priority. In turnings and dividends. The reason for the share classification is to provide a strong founder with continued control of the business and at the same time, allowing them to go to public Capital markets for growth capital. Most small businesses just have one class of common shares; any number of shares owned by individuals determine their level of ownership.

Preferred Equity

Preferred equity is a special class of equity that can have equity- and debt-like characteristics. An example of preferred equity is the position that Warren Buffett took in 2008 in Goldman Sachs. Rather than buying common shares in the investment bank, his multibillion-dollar investment came as preferred equity with a 10% dividend. Preferred equity provides a way for investors to set up special investment characteristics while leaving the original share structure without any changes. The special characteristics can include special dividends, special rights thresholds for buyback of the equity by the company as well as features to convert the investment into other types of investment.

Convertible Equity

A convertible equity is any type of equity that has the feature change from one type to another. Typically, the convertible feature is part of a preferred equity where the preferred portion can convert into a certain number of common shares. The feature gives the investor the option to take advantage of the dividend feature of the preferred share or if the common stock takes off in value converting and getting the common share gains. Let's say in the case of our preferred stock, there is a 10% dividend and the option to convert to a particular number of shares. If the company was to offer a public offering, the preferred investor might see a better return by converting from the preferred to common shares and participating in the public offering.

Warrants

Warrants are typically a feature of debt and provide the debt provider with the opportunity to retire some or all the debt for an equity position. Some mezzanine debt providers will ask for warrants as a feature to the debt they provide; this gives them the option to convert the debt to equity, thereby giving the investment more flexibility an opportunity for a higher return.

Capital Accounts & Units

The capital account is how LLCs and partnerships track the paid in and distributed equity for pass-through entities.

If you're a husband and wife team, you are likely to form the business with a 50/50 share, and the profits will eventually flow to a single tax return but if your partnership is with another individual it will be important to track differences in the amount of paid in capital and distributions. One of the strengths of the LLC structure is just this feature that you can have any capital divisions and member structure you can imagine.

TERMS ASSOCIATED WITH EQUITY

Dilution

Dilution is a feature of equity anytime a company takes in more equity and issues shares in support of the issuance; the number of shares in the pool increases and therefore all shareholders have their portion adjusted accordingly. As the original owner of the business with 100% equity, if you were to take an outside investment of $1 million and they valued your business at $2 million, then your position would be diluted by 50%.

Capital Calls

In closely held businesses, when there is a need for additional capital for growth that will come in the form of equity, there will be what is known as a call for capital. The business makes the request to investors to provide their proportional share of the call within a designated timeframe. This is typically outlined in the operating agreement. As a member, you have the choice to provide your pro-rata share or be diluted based on the final funds contributed.

For most, you will not have the need for a complex equity structure, given you will be the sole owner. If you are in a partnership, you should have written agreement on how equity is handled when additional equity needs to come into to the business as to how it is handled. If one of the partners is not able to contribute capital and the other is having, a system for contribution and dilution will lessen the chances of hard feelings.

As far as sources of equity go, the main one we have been focusing on is you as the owner-investor. Following, we will explore the process of bootstrapping a business further as well as giving information on other sources of equity along with the pros and cons that come with them.

SOURCES OF EQUITY

Retained Earnings

The best organic source of equity is from the profits of the business staying in the business as working capital.

Boot Strap

We discussed in start up the differences in funding a business yourself and seeking other people's money. Making a business work with little capital or conversely getting other people to invest both have pros and cons. The reality is, more businesses self-fund than source equity elsewhere during start-up and early years of operation. So, how do you go about doing it?

The real trick to bootstrapping is aligning growth expectations with the funds you can contribute to the business and that the business will generate after it begins to operate.

I was involved in a bootstrap start-up with three other partners. We set the expectations where everyone was clear on the amount of work required of those that was employed at day jobs and when revenues started to come in, how we would have team members exit their day jobs to our new business. We also worked out how we were going to handle actual cash contributions, given not all the partners were able to make equal contributions. If you will have partners, it is worthwhile to look at pay, contribution and equity and define this in the operating agreement. If you're not sure about what each person's share should be then define what the different types of contribution will earn. It is important to set expectations for what contributed capital gets a partner what effort gets a partner and most importantly what amount of working capital is needed to execute the plan.

Once we all agreed to the rules this influenced our planning for the business. We knew that with only so much up front capital we could only have two partners leave to join the business in the beginning and then how we were to invest the profits we generated back into the business to grow it. Our initial work discussing our complex partnership help us to understand how best to use our limited capital and set realistic expectations for the partners.

Iterative Planning

You could just say "damn the torpedoes" and plow ahead with your venture. Having that level of commitment and enthusiasm is great but let's strike a balance between planning and action to mitigate your risk and improve your chances of success.

Begin with a business plan—laying out a realistic plan aligned with the time you will dedicate to the project. If you are starting out as a side deal and will continue to work a day job, then your personal plan for income and the need to generate income immediately is reduced but the amount of time you can commit is lower.

Business

If your plan is a slower rolling start, then you can model out less upfront capital and design your plan in a way where the business profits roll back in to provide the necessary growth capital. If, however, you believe that your plan requires more of your time to get momentum, then you need to determine the duration of negative cash flow and build up a reserve of cash to support you through the initial cash flow burn. My experience is, what you will really need is 1.5 -2x what you project in your plan. If you choose to not build up that level of cash, expect to be looking for funding later when you need to be focusing on the business instead.

The key to iterative planning is understanding the asumptions you made in the plan and when you begin to see the actual results against the plan you adjust. If the sales are happening on schedule but customers take longer to pay then you may slow down new sales inititives. Conversely if your efforts deliver more capital you can adjust to grow faster. Have part of your plan to revist the plan and adjust to a second an third iteration as you get real results. You don't get extra points for getting the plan right the first time the plan is a tool to help you navigate risk.

Personal

Your personal situation will determine the options you have for how to start your business. You really need to scrutinize your personal finances and understand the costs associated with starting a business. If you have a spouse or partner that provides income to your household, then you have more latitude, but if you are the primary source of income, you need to plan carefully for all the expenses. For example, you need to consider any fringe benefits that may go away when you quit, like health insurance. Many first-time entrepreneurs don't figure in the added costs that need to be built into the plan.

None of what I am covering here should be taken as words of discouragement but rather guidance as to plan for the funding for both you and the business. The moral of the story is: you will be trading off time for money. You will need to wait longer to exit your day job or hold off on hiring someone if you don't have the cash and require the business to generate it. Accepting this and planning accordingly will make you far more efficient because you will be focused on a workable, realistic plan that will likely deliver results sooner because you won't be wasting time trying to raise money.

Private Investment

The other source for equity investment for both early stage operations and established ventures is private investment. To help understand the sources and requirements associated with the various types of funding, I find it helpful to discuss Early Stage Money and growth/buyout capital. The investors have very different risk profiles and investment focuses. Many early investors also provide additional mentoring and guidance to help you be successful. With these investors, they will expect you to be able to pitch them on the deal and answer the following questions.

What is the problem you solve for customers?

What is the size addressable market?

What is the amount of funds needed?

How will the funds be used?

What do they get for their investment? When will they get their money back?

What will the return be on that money?

The following list of private investor types will have different profiles of how and when they invest they will all ask the questions above and your ability to answer them is the single biggest factor in your securing funding.

A short note on Valuation

At some point, an investor is looking to equate the investment they will make in a portion of the business, and this establishes the businesses value. You likely have seen this on shark tank where the entrepreneur says "I am seeking $100,000 for 10% of the business." That means they feel the business is worth one million dollars. Be realistic in your valuation. If you don't have revenues, you have a tough time justifying the valuation. Established businesses that are profitable command valuations between 4-12 times EBITDA. So, if a business that generates $250,000 in EBITDA can also be worth one million dollars, you really need to have a compelling story to get million dollar valuations.

Here are some of the types and sources of private equity investment

Accelerators & Incubators

Incubators are focused on helping entrepreneurs to get their business concept to the point of being viable for public launch. Usually, no money is provided, but they do support you with mentors and resources that can help to get you organized and moving in the right direction.

Accelerators provide a process to entrepreneurs to get their business idea formalized and get to a minimum viable product. Every major city has an accelerator program.

Companies are vetted by a committee and admitted into the program where they get use of a co-share facility, mentorship, and run through a program to prepare them to pitch to investors. Graduates would get some money and give up 8-10% of the business for the time in the program and any cash. The other expectation is that the program has helped the founders prepare to secure additional funds and will introduce the founders to potential investors. For the business to succeed and the Accelerator to make money there will need to be future funding rounds.

Time has shown that the results of these programs are very low yield and many programs have been changing the model to award investment as the entrepreneurs build out a viable business. While these programs can lead to introductions to bigger investors and certainly help you to get your act together, you immediately lose some equity for getting through the program.

All the programs are very lean in their investment, and you will likely need to have some other means of support while in the program.

Angel Investing

Angel investors can be a single investor or a formal group. In the case of a group, they typically have guidelines for the types of investments they make and the amounts they invest. They will be expecting 8-12% of the business equity for a small amount of money; this money is typically enough to test out the thesis of the business but not enough get you to a larger round of financing.

Seed Funds

Many universities run programs where entrepreneurs can present ideas in a venture challenge to get some seed money. This money is usually given without any strings attached but, again, is not a significant amount of capital.

In any of the above situations where funds are awarded to your enterprise, and there is not a request for equity, the funds need to be treated as income and will attract income tax.

Venture Capital

Venture capital firms are very diverse in the types of investing they do and the stage that they make investments. While getting venture capital is an option, you will be spending the time to garner the investment and then expect to give up a large portion of the company to investors. It may not all be at once, but for a venture capital company to make money, they need to see your business succeed and do so quickly; they may decide to take a more aggressive investment position and put more men in to scale up the operation. Each time this is done, the founders will be diluted down further. Even if the founders have a significant or majority position now, VC firm will let their investment be left without controls. There will be a board, and there will be a tilt of voting rights to their capital.

Private Equity

Growth Capital

If you are a business that has been operating for some time, profitable and can really grow but lack the working capital to take advantage of the opportunities in front of you, there may be options for significant outside investment.

There is nearly seven hundred and fifty billion dollars of investment money looking to make private equity investments, with the majority looking for a place in the buyout or growth segment of the market. The majority will be placed in the middle market, but there is a growing number of firms that are considering small business for firms they can help grow.

Most look to have a control position but also need to have a solid management team to run the business.

They desire good management and a solid business with some competitive advantages.

What they offer:

Financing

This is meaningful; many businesses never reach their full potential because the owner doesn't have the capital needed to grow the business. Trading off 100% ownership in a smaller venture for a smaller share of a larger venture is usually a better option, but the reality is, you may get two or three liquidity opportunities. For example, if you have a solid business with some competitive advantage and choose to sell a majority portion of the business, you get a payout now plus you now have, say, 40% of a well-capitalized operation with a board of knowledgeable advisors. If you work together for 4-5 years to grow the business, they will be looking to a second equity event where you will get a chance to sell another chunk of your equity but now of a much larger entity.

Individual Investors

There are wealthy investors—usually, past entrepreneurs—that look to invest as minority or majority stakeholders in businesses. If you look to outside individual investors, make sure that you have solid written agreements around the transaction and future rights. A minority shareholder can be just as much trouble as one that has a major stake.

Family Offices

Wealthy investors sometimes run an independent investment office to manage their wealth. Rather than trusting investment professionals, they build a team that can manage, preserve, and grow wealth.

Many of these offices invest in small businesses indirectly through private equity or directly through a fund they manage. The great thing about family offices is, they are looking for long-term wealth creation and are usually patient investors looking to see a long relationship with the companies they put money to work with. Finding a family office that is interested in your space can be a great investor with deep pockets and strong community connections.

DEBT

We talked about, in buying a business, about how a seller could be a possible provider of debt in the purchase of a business. While debt is commonly used in the purchase of a business to reduce the amount of equity needed, debt is most often used to fund working capital needs of a business. Rather than focusing on the uses of debt, we will explore what debt is and various sources of debt for your business.

Debt is a form of financing where the owner of the capital (the lender) provides you with cash, with an obligation that you will pay back the initial sum (principal) and interest. The benefit for the lender is, the capital they provide you will generate a return and grow in value.

The benefit to the borrower is that the principal, while part of the company capital structure, is categorized as a liability and not equity. If the terms of payment are met, the lender has no claims against the business assets like equity does.

Debt usually has a lower cost of capital than equity. First, it typically carries a lower interest rate, and even when it does not, it benefits from the interest rate expense deduction and associated tax rate to deliver a lower cost of capital. From the perspective of ownership, the benefit is, debt providers don't look to be an owner in the business; the lender is an investor in that they are betting that you and your business have a high likelihood of paying off the debt from the cash flows generated by the business. They further hedge the risk by having claims to assets if a default takes place or the business begins to fail to meet certain ratios.

Lenders are not typically looking to become owners; they are seeking lower risk reward scenarios to generate income from capital. A good example of debt is the mortgage on your home; it is a debt instrument but used to purchase your house secured by the underlying asset. The lender expects a low, stable return with a low default rate, and if there is a default, the expectation is that all or most of the loan will be recovered through the sale of the underlying asset (collateral), with the borrower losing equity value they had in the asset.

Most debts have some type of backstop for the debt provider to recover the loss of capital. They use collateral, some asset of the owner or the business. It can be the accounts receivable, inventory, specific business assets, or a loan associated with personal assets like your home.

Sometimes the lender will seek a personal guarantee. Once you signed one, you no longer have the personal protection provided by your company against that creditor. If the business defaults, they can go to court and go after you and your personal assets that have been pledged to collect any lost collateral.

Debt comes in a wide range of forms from you using your personal credit card to finance your business through more complex forms like mezzanine debt or factoring. Following is some insights into the different types and uses of debt:

Credit Cards

Credit cards are the most used form of debt in the startup and operation of small business, making movies, and publishing of books.

The most common cards used are those that are the personal cards held by the owner, followed by cards issued to the company.

Personal Guarantee

When reviewing your credit card agreement for a business credit card, most credit card companies will look to get the owner to sign a personal guaranty for the credit card. By doing so, if you were to file for bankruptcy, the credit card company would have the option to pursue you personally for any unpaid balance, with your only options being to pay the balance or to file for a personal bankruptcy to protect yourself from those creditors that hold personal guarantees. Keep this in mind when dealing with ANY credit for your business of loan documents you sign. If you agree to personal guarantee, your liability to creditors is not limited by the bounds of the corporation you have set up

Appropriate use of credit cards can help you to finance your business and improve your businesses working capital situation. Without using the credit balance of the card and paying it off monthly, you benefit from the card in two ways. First, you will improve your cash flow by picking up twenty-one to thirty days to collect cash prior to having to outlay cash; secondly, credit cards become an excellent method for tracking expenses if you are not using some other system. It was also demonstrated in the cost of capital section that using the credit given to you on your credit card and carrying a balance increases your working capital and likely (depending on the interest rate) could deliver a lower cost of capital alternative to your business.

Even the smallest start-up can access outside capital if the owner has access to a credit card. The real trick is not so much the access but to have a plan that effectively uses the small pool of capital to generate a cash flow more than the cost of capital in the pool, thereby creating more capital to fuel the business growth. The use of outside capital, however small, is more important for business formation and growth than the size of the capital pool.

To put credit card debt and owner equity into context the numbers below compare the amount of equity in the business other than credit card debt, meaning they have put cash in the business prior to adding credit card debt Here are some numbers:

The top 25% of businesses have equity of $3,017 and Personal credit card debt of $3,651. The bottom 25% have equity of $1,497 and credit card debt of $2,793, providing a range of 1:1 to 1:2 equity to debt based on owner equity contribution and debt held on personally guaranteed cards. You should strive for a 1:1 or lower debt ratio.

This combination of cash and credit card debt is really considered all owners' equity in that the owner is on the hook if the debt is from a personally guaranteed card. The advantage is sourcing a larger pool of capital and with the tax shield, a lower cost of capital (the business deducts the interest expense).

Since the banking crisis of 2008, credit cards have been the way most banks expend credit to businesses in their formative years. It provides them with a low-cost system for operating the credit line that is suitable for most businesses and gives the bank a good return. Commercial Banks do, however, offer other types of loans.

When setting up your business accounts at any bank, you can request to set up a business credit card. Because your business is new, the credit card provider (it may not be your bank) may ask for a personal guarantee. The guarantee could also be in the fine print; make sure you read it. Once this guarantee is in place, it won't go away; therefore, to work on limiting liability, I recommend to, instead, use an existing personal credit card for the business. You will need to track company-related purchases and the associated credit balances and interest payments to charge against the business.

It may be easier to get a new personal credit card issued that you will use only for the business. You still have the same personal liability, but you are not associating a personal guarantee with the company and its liabilities.

This credit card, although used solely for your business, is technically a personal credit card but since it is dedicated to the business, you know that all items are tied to the operation of the business for simplified record keeping.

Later, when your business has a history of profitability, you can look to get company credit cards issues. Don't confuse debt cards that your bank issues when you open an account for your business as a credit card. While they will act more like a credit card at restaurants and paying for expenses, there is no credit function and what you "charge" will be deducted from your business checking account in a few days.

What will a bank look for to issue company credit cards?

- One to three years of operation.
- Copies of financials.
- Copies of tax returns on the business.
- If the business has not shown a profit, then it will be harder to secure credit without a personal guarantee.

The issuance of company credit cards is also a stepping stone to a commercial loan from a bank. Part of getting access to commercial debt is a deliberate process by you to demonstrate your business being creditworthy, including business profitability and low or no balance on your credit card.

401K Loan

One good source of debt where you have control is taking a loan from your 401K. While you do need to fill out paperwork and there are rules and regulations around taking a loan, it is a great source for you to get access to capital.

The main reason is that this is a loan that you pay back to yourself. Any interest can be deducted as an expense on the business yet the interest goes back to you on a tax-deferred basis. There are limits to the amount you can withdraw, and there is a fixed timeframe for payback of the loan but most 401Ks have a fast and easy process for doing a loan, and with a cap of $50,000, you can get a solid chunk of funding without a huge approval process.

Just because a 401K loan can be an easy process should not let you out of the responsibility of doing the legwork to demonstrate that the business plan is worthy of the loan. Time for the alter egos of operator and investor to kick in and make sure that you do your due diligence on the investment and return before drawing the funds.

If you decide to do this, you can check with your company HR department or whoever handles your 401K plan where you work. Keep in mind this is your money; you do not have to disclose to them what you are using it for nor do they have a say in your access to it. The loan rules and regulations are very clear and part of the plan document that they legally need to provide you.

Prior to getting into commercial debt, it will be helpful to review some common terms and concepts.

Secured credit

Secured credit is an obligation that lender gets as part of terms of the loan. Like a home or car loan, the loan is collateralized with the underlying asset the loan is used to fund. There are several other types of collateral used to secure loans for businesses; it can be specific assets like equipment, the business itself as well as the accounts receivable and inventory of the business.

Financial Covenants

These are rules set by a lender within the loan documents that can trigger a default of the loan agreement even if you are current with the loans interest and principle payments. Lenders typically include these ratio covenants to provide them more latitude if the financial health of the firm looks questionable.

Asset based lending—where hard assets are used as the security of the loan, the case may be that these are business assets like machine tools, vehicles, or computer hardware. A loan to asset value ratio is set to assure that the collateral value supports recovery of the loan principle if there is a default.

Cash flow based Lending is where the loan is collateralized by the businesses inventory and accounts receivable. This type of loan is traditionally a **credit line** that adjusts in the **base of borrowing** between zero and some high credit limit but is always tethered to current inventory and accounts receivable. The borrowing base formula is designed so that if the accounts receivable is collected and the inventory sold, the loan will be covered. To do this, the lender assigns ratios to the A/R and inventory to assure the cash flow covers the loan. Typically, inventory is at 50% and receivables between 50 and 80%.

Since 2008, commercial bank loans have been harder to secure. There are less regional banks with a focus on small business, and those that are still active have far more compliance issues because of the Frank-Dodd act, making for more expensive loan administration. The result is that commercial bank credit is tougher to secure.

A study completed by the National Center for the Middle Market and the Milken Institute showed that in the previous three years, 30% of companies did not seek any capital and of those that did, the majority was via a commercial bank loan. Those that did not use commercial banks did their financing through a range of private and public sources.

When should you consider using a commercial bank for a loan?

Your business is profitable and has a positive cash flow, but there is seasonality or lags in cash flow. You could need to build up inventory for a selling season or new client growth.

What will the bank expect from you?

- Two to three years of financials.
- Business tax returns that tie off to the financials.
- Your plan for the use of cash, including how the business is impacted by the loan—if cash flow based needs explain the purpose and if asset based loans explain why the equipment is needed.

The old line is, banks are willing to loan you money if you don't need it. There is some truth to it, but a bank will have an easier time if you provide a well-thought plan for the uses of the funds and present it so the loan officer can sell your case to the loan committee.

Local commercial banks

Focus on asset-based lending, real estate and cash flow based lending for the most part. Most local commercial banks are actively seeking customers to establish working relationships. The key is understanding the size and types of loans the bank is comfortable making. The large banks where you may start out your business accounts because you already have a personal account tend to treat small businesses like personal accounts and won't extend credit beyond a credit card facility. Small business loans are not a sweet spot for them, and they focus on larger loans that are more profitable and can support the costs that big banks have. Smaller community banks tend to do better with small business loans that are ranging from $50,000 up to ten million.

Referral is always the best place to start, so look for other business owners and ask them who they use and what it is like working with the bank they work with.

If your company needs larger loans to grow, then you must plan and begin to develop a relationship with a bank before you need the money. Most business owners have poor relationships with the banking process because they start looking for a loan after it is too late and associate the pain of an underfunded business with the slow banking process. Instead, start meeting and talking with bankers proactively to help them learn about you and your business. Use your meetings to build a relationship and ask their guidance as to what they will need from you and when to get a loan approved.

This process builds the rapport with the bank and gives you time to evaluate who you like to work with. Having a good relationship with a banker that is engaged and learning about your customers and how you serve them will help as your business grows and changes.

You also need to understand that a loan decision is made by a committee, so the more you can learn about the process and help your banker to present your needs in the best light, the easier it will be for you to get the loan when it is needed.

Finally, the perception that you are proactive and a planner getting the work done well before the actual loan is needed will make you an attractive prospect that will get more banks interested and get an easier approval.

Using what you have learned in the financial command section, you can present your capital structure and working capital needs in an easy-to-understand way to the bank and show that you are knowledgeable in the use of debt as a financial tool and have thought out the impacts and risk associated with the loan request.

Mezzanine Debt Providers

Mezzanine Debt is typically used in middle market businesses as an alternative source to commercial banks. The lender has less regulation because they are not a bank and have flexibility as to the types of loans and the purpose of the loan. Private equity uses mezzanine debt in the leveraged buyout of businesses. When buying a business, they provide a portion of the purchase price as equity, and the rest, they borrow from a mezzanine firm; the reason is, the Mez firm will take a subordinate position to any secured commercial debt from a bank.

Priority	Rate	Use	Owner
1	Libor+1%	Line of Credit	Bank
2	Prime +2.5%	Buyout	Mezz Firm

The purpose of this structure is to get a better return by using less equity and having the business cash flows pay off the debt. While this is considered financial engineering, it is not different from what you can do as a business owner with debt to get better returns on your equity.

While most readers will not have a need for these types of firms, you should know about them. There are firms looking for smaller businesses to loan to, and they are more flexible than a bank and offer options to financing that most people are not aware of.

Factoring

Factoring is a method of funding working capital using unfulfilled purchase orders as the collateral for the loan.

Factoring is very common in industries like fashion where orders are received in advance, and payments need to be made to manufacturers. The factoring company pays a portion of the contract in advance to the borrower and then collects the full amount of the contract—the difference being the cost of capital to borrow the money.

To facilitate a factored deal, there is a lock box set up with the factoring company of a bank where the funds are deposited by the purchaser, and the factoring company gets first claim on the funds so that they are assured of payment.

One concept some companies have about using factoring is, it can create additional paperwork for the buyer. In many industries, the use of factoring is commonplace, and there is no stigma, but in other industries, the use of factoring can be seen as an inconvenience to a customer to an issue of liquidity of the supplier.

Since 2008, commercial credit has been harder to get for small businesses, and more companies are accessing factoring. It can be a good supplementary short-term solution for your business to deal with growth from big orders. Where it can take banks months or years to get comfortable giving you the credit you need, a factoring company is used to making decisions in days based on the credit worthiness of your customer and confidence in your ability to supply, given you have the necessary working capital.

If you would like to learn more about factoring and get contacts that can fund your growth, then follow this link

SBA Loans

The Small Business Administration offers several loan guarantee programs to support small businesses. The SBA does not make the loans but provides a guarantee on your behalf to the lender. There are several debt-related programs and some equity-related programs all facilitated by private third parties that participate in the SBA programs.

Only around 5% of businesses ever pursue and complete an SBA loan. The reasons given in the Milken Study for not using the SBA were:

21% of respondents said the process was too difficult and bureaucratic

19% were unaware of the options the SBA provides

15% said the terms were too onerous

10% said the process took too long

9% said the funding did not meet the company needs

8% found better terms elsewhere

My observation is that SBA programs do provide opportunity but come with rules and regulations that you must accept. There are good programs that help with the financing of buildings for a business, but general growth loans typically come with the owner having to pledge assets like their home.

The link below provides a search system to connect business owners up to different providers and the products they support. If you are looking to raise funds, it does not hurt to explore SBA-backed financing there are rated and program benefits to be had.

https://www.sba.gov/tools/linc

Just as many businesses don't like the extra paperwork, the same goes for banks. Below is a list of the top SBA lenders; this is a good place to source an SBA loan, and in the case of most of the banks, they have extra resources in place to help you with your application.

Here is a link to the top 100 SBA lenders:

https://www.sba.gov/lenders-top-100

Don't be surprised if you bring up the idea of an SBA loan to your local banker and they tell you to look elsewhere. Small banks shy away from the extra regulation and work because they don't find that the government guarantee is all that helpful in risk mitigation.

There are consultants that help businesses to get these types of loans. They are not the loan facilitator or lender but know of the various banks that make these types of loans. The consultant charges a fee—usually, a percentage of the loan they secure for the business.

CROWD FUNDING

A recent development for fundraising is using a crowdfunding source like Kickstarter and Indigogo.

The interesting feature of crowdfunding is, the people that pledge money do not have an interest in getting equity in the business; they are more focused on getting early access to your product and service. This presents you with a great opportunity to do to key things in the startup of a venture:

1. Validate that there is a minimum viable audience.

2. Get the capital to bring a product to market.

Using a platform like Kickstarter to validate your idea is phenomenal. As we will discuss in online presence and marketing, you can have a virtual operation and present your concept to the market and determine the market interest and willingness to pay for your new product even before you make the first one.

At the School of the Art Institute of Chicago, they run a design studio where they help the student develop designs and then go to Kickstarter to launch the idea. The truth is, a lot of them end up being duds and never get funded but there have been some wild successes where students have taken a school project and, through this process, established a business. They get two things every business needs: money and a connection with customers.

My experience is that Kickstarter is very good for product-based companies. People on Kickstarter are prepared to pay in advance for a new cool product and be an early adopter. The other thing that is great about Kickstarter is that the funds you raise have no cap. Go and see for yourself; there are folks raising $500 and others raising $500,000.

To successfully run a Kickstarter campaign, you need to prepare an excellent marketing program and actively work to sell your product. You can see that the successful campaigns have videos, content, and a story to get a person excited about the product. You also need to have a solid understanding of your cost to manufacture. You need to price your pledges in a way that you can deliver the products you promise and end up with some profit to grow the business with.

Kickstarter takes 10% of the funds you receive so make sure that cost is built into your business plan and what you need to raise in your campaign.

Tax implications

The funds you receive from your Kickstarter campaign are taxable as income. Of course, you deduct your cost of goods and expenses to come up with the actual net income that is taxable, but I have seen a few people that forget that there is a tax implication with the pledges.

A recommendation is to set up your company and get a separate tax id and use the company's tax id for your Kickstarter campaign.

RATIOS YOU SHOULD KNOW

SOME OWNERS HAVE an aversion to learning the various business ratios and what they can tell about a business. It doesn't help that ratios have arcane terms that might add to further confusion. These ratios are your friends, and when understood and used appropriately, you will be able to get a better feel for what is going on in your business and have insight into how changes are influencing your ability to grow. These ratios are another set of tools for your financial command of the business. They help you to evaluate performance and show others how your business is performing.

A good practice is to calculate these quarterly if you are just getting familiar with them. Another practice is to use some of these ratios as Key Performance Indicators and track them monthly using tools like a trailing twelve-month average

Ratios

Here is a list of the most common ratios, how they are calculated, and when to use them. The ratios help you to measure business performance and catch subtle changes that could compound to cause real problems. Later, you will see in working capital and the sales trough examples where growth has sucked up cash. In the examples provided, all were optimum in the sense that the business parameters did not change and the only variable was customer addition but what happens if in the midst of adding these new customers, your gross margins drop by one percentage point, your inventory turns decrease by one turn, and your customers slip in days outstanding by two days? Could you figure out what that additional cash drain would be? Ratios can help you to see these problems and fix them sooner.

If you see you're having an issue with inventory turns, you can assess it quickly and then determine if you need to work out a deal with a vendor to increase inventory or cut back on some pending orders to stop inventory from building well before you find out all your working capital is tied up in your inventory.

How to use ratios

On their own, they are meaningless. To use them well, you need to look at them like business or historical performance of your business. Since they are based on your accounting practices, if you do not keep accurate up- to -date accounts, your ratios will suffer.

Gross Profit Margin is measured by looking at the remaining profit from a sale after the cost of goods is removed. Gross Margin is a core ratio that should be understood and used to evaluate how much profit is created above your basic service or product. Without healthy gross margins you can not support operating expenses.

$$Gross\ Profit = \frac{Revenue - Cost\ of\ Good\ Sold}{Revenue}$$

Operating Expense ratio is the percentage of your revenue that is consumed by operations.

$$Operating\ Expense\ \% = \frac{Operating\ Expenses}{Revenue}$$

Operating Profit is the profit after you subtract operating expenses from gross profit.

Returns Measurement

The following are different returns measurements:

Return on Assets = Net Income / Total Assets

The return on assets is a measurement of how well the business utilizes assets to create more assets. Businesses with high return on assets warrant further investment into assets.

Return on Equity = Net Income / Total Equity

The return on equity is a measurement of how well the business performs for its shareholders. You can use this measurement to determine if the business warrants further investment of equity.

Cash on Cash

One simple measurement that is used for determining an investment's performance is cash on cash return. It is simple. You invested five dollars and later they gave you back twelve dollars—that would be a 2.4x return. This measurement is usually calculated before taxes are paid and does not have any function of time. That return could be in a year or ten years from now; it is still the same CoC return.

Internal Rate of Return or Return on Investment

Internal rate of return provides a time-related function to give a measurement of how fast an investment increases.

If you invest five dollars and get back twelve dollars in one year, then the internal rate of return is 140%, but if it occurred over ten years, then it is a 9% IRR. The easiest way to calculate an IRR is to use the IRR formula in excel.

You should set IRR goals for your business. If you put $1,000 into the business and set the goal to take that $1,500 out as a capital distribution, two years later, you would have achieved a minimum 22.4% return; the return is higher because your business is still running, and you own all that value.

As the owner, you might look to modify this ratio and include your post payroll, benefits, and discretionary earnings to evaluate your personal return on equity.

If you wonder what is a better way to weigh return, I suggest IRR as it evaluates the term of the investment along with the return.

Liquidity

These ratios show a firm's ability to meet short-term financial obligations. They are of interest to business operators and those extending short-term credit to the firm and to the owner to evaluate the state of working capital in the business.

Current Ratio (working capital Ratios) = current assets / current liabilities

One drawback to the current ratio is that inventory may include items that are not easy to liquidate.

Quick Ratios = (Current Assets- Inventory) / current liabilities

This ratio only looks at liquid assets like cash and receivables against liabilities

Cash Ratio = (Cash + Marketable Securities) / Current Liabilities

This ratio only looks at cash versus liabilities and is the best of all the ratios given. If you get into a tight spot, collecting receivables or liquidating inventory can be time-consuming. To put inventory and receivables into perspective, most lenders, when determining your borrowing base, will only give you 50% credit for inventory and 80% for receivables if they feel your counter party is of high credit worthiness.

Asset Turnover Ratios

Turnover ratios indicate the performance of your assets. How well does the business generate more cash from the cash invested into assets like equipment and inventory?

Receivables Turnover = Annual Credit sales / accounts receivable

The receivables turnover indicates how quickly credit sales are collected.

Average Collection Period = Accounts Receivable / (Annual Credit Sales /365)

Sometimes referred to as days to collection or collection period. This indicates the time it takes to collect a credit sale. This ratio can be applied to the business to determine overall ability to collect as well as for each customer to determine their payment performance.

Compare each customer's collection period to the company's average to see who your slow paying customers are and track each client's average collection to highlight changes in payment behavior. This is a key indicator to a client having cash problems.

Inventory Turnover = Cost of Goods Sold / Current Inventory

This is an indicator of the business's utilization of the inventory. The higher the ratio, the better, and it indicates your ability to turn your hard assets into cash.

Inventory Period = Average Inventory / (Average cost of goods sold/365)

This ratio gives you guidance as to how many days it takes to turn inventory into cash. Keep in mind the true inventory to cash cycle is the inventory period + the collection period. Watching the inventory period and collection period is important when your business is inventory intensive and growing. Your working capital problems will compound if while your sales grow, either or both periods begin to increase.

Financial Ratios

These are very important for lenders to assure that the business assets that secure the loan can support the repayment of the loan and if the case is that you cannot service the loan, that there is a good chance that they will recover their capital through the sale of the assets of the business that are collateral for the loan.

Debt Ratio = Total Debt / Total Assets

Debt to Equity = Total Debt / Total Equity

Interest Coverage = EBITDA/ Interest payments

This ratio shows the firm's ability to service the interest obligation for the debt.

Key Performance Indicators and Reports

Ratios can be key performance indicators. A ratio becomes a key performance indicator when you, as the owner, choose to use it as a key tool for your business operation. You work on a regular basis to continually improve the measurement. Take Gross Margin, for example; if you monitor it monthly and work to hold your margins at or above a certain threshold, it is acting as a key performance indicator.

Here are some tools that can help you to better measure business performance rather than just looking at a ratio as a snapshot you can use these tools to see trends:

Trailing twelve-month average

This is a fantastic way to measure sales, expenses, and profit. You add the current month to the previous eleven months to come up with a number. In the case of sales, you can use the gross annual number or divide it by twelve to get a better feel for monthly performance.

It removes seasonality

It smooths the indicator

You can pair a trailing twelve month with a trailing three month or a trailing thirty-six month to be able to visualize short term and long term trends and evaluate your business performance at a whole new level.

A great tool is to use the three-year average and the one-year average and chart them as line charts on the same chart. If you see the twelve-month drop below the thirty-six month for more than a month or two and stay there, then you know there is something beyond a seasonal blip that needs to be addressed. Now it could be that you had a large one-off order that has fallen off the twelve-month so you know quickly what the cause for the drop is but if it is not that obvious, you need to start digging to see what is sucking the growth out of the business.

PRODUCTIVITY AND AUTOMATION

THIS SECTION IS about putting as much of your business on autopilot as possible and using information technology to serve your customer and make your new venture look professional. As an operator of multiple businesses over a period of twenty years, I am amazed at what can be done with cloud-based software and desktop computing power. What required tens or hundreds of thousands of dollars in the past now can be done for several hundred dollars of fees each month. The biggest boon for a business owner is how these software as service options elevate the need for consultants or staff to come and fix computer issues that in the past would disrupt your business.

For those of you just starting, this is a fantastic advantage because you do not have the capital requirements that were needed in the past for IT. Better still is that you can get much of this up and running from a home office and maybe even without needing a computer, essentially running your entire business from a phone or tablet.

With all the suggestions I provide in this section, I will discuss options that will allow you to scale up and minimize cost. The approach I usually take is to start with free or low monthly service fee and then scale up as needed to learn if the service is worthwhile and keeping costs to a minimum.

Domain Name

A domain name may be more important than your company name. Having a catchy short domain name that resonates with your prospects is fundamental to marketing your business. Even before you incorporate your business, get the appropriate domain name for your business if you plan to have an online presence. Today it is hard to think of a business that does not need to have some minimal presence online to help customers to do their initial research on your company and build confidence in doing business with you. A minimum threshold for your business should be an email address that has a professional domain versus a public domain like Hotmail or Gmail. The next level being a simple landing page to provide contact information and give a simple introduction to how you benefit a customer.

So, if you are looking to get a domain name that is your business name, your personal name, or a catch phrase that captures your product or service, then you will need to secure a domain name. There are a few ways to get a domain name. You can go to network solutions https://www.networksolutions.com and buy just the domain name. This is also a good place to go to search for open domain names to find one that is the right fit for your venture.

I have found the best deals are when you are signing up for other services like web hosting or email services where they include the domain name as part of the service. Do some research because most domain providers deeply discount the first year, and then charge more in following years, as they know you have invested in the development of the domain and won't want to lose it.

To determine how and where to stake your digital claim, you need to define what you are trying to do with your business online.

What does your business need to have online to support customers and present your business in a positive light?

This list outlines the most common needs:

- Email & Document Sharing Only
- Billboard & Simple Marketing
- E-Commerce
- Custom Online Presence
- Ability for customers to self-serve and seek content

Email & Document Sharing

If you don't need to have a web presence but use tools like word processing, email, and spreadsheet programs, then an option is to set up with google docs (now G Suite) or Microsoft Office 365. With both, you can choose to buy a domain name when you set up your account, thereby assuring your email has a business domain rather than Hotmail, yahoo, or google.

G Suite

With G Suite, you get a word processing, spreadsheet, and presentation software along with email, calendar, video conferencing, and cloud storage.

G Suite has always had a focus on collaboration and provides one of the best means to work remotely. G Suite also has a significant number of plug-ins to other programs to make the package interact better. The typical fee for the G suite is $5 a month.

Added benefit to G suite is that there is a huge library of mail and calendar plugins to integrate Gmail with other software you may use, including customer relationship management systems or project management tools.

Office 365

This Microsoft product provides you with the standard office products you may be used to and gives you the flexibility to work in desktop or collaborate in the cloud. The product also includes a significant amount of cloud storage to house your files. It is more expensive than G suite, but you do get the full desktop versions of products like Excel, Word, PowerPoint and others and the ability to use ii on multiple devices and a TB of online storage through one drive. You also get HD video conferencing via Skype with the business level account.

File Storage

When thinking about files storage, you will need to think about files you need and files you need to serve up to customers. In most cases, you can use a system that is capable of doing both. You will need to be assured that there are the appropriate levels of protection to keep your files under password protection and your clients can have their files also protected.

The advent of cloud-based storage has provided businesses with a significant reduction in cost and increase in productivity. No longer does a business need a network and attached storage for the business to operate. Cloud storage also expedited file compatibility, allowing for just about any device to be able to view and edit a file.

Most businesses require some internal file exchange and storage even if you are the only employee. Having a file system in place where you can get to your files from any location and from multiple devices will make you more productive. Here are some options:

Dropbox

This is a good platform for file storage. It provides the ability to scale as your business grows and features to control file access. If you were part of the promotions, you might have 5-10 gigabytes of free space to store files on. If you did not get a free account back when Dropbox was making such to capture customers, you would have to sign up for a paid account. While I still use it, I find it tough to pay for this service that I can get it included with G suite or Office 365.

ICloud

Apple users get 5 GB of space with an iCloud account. If you are backing up your devices to iCloud, then this space goes quickly. Like other services, you can pay to get more space.

Google Drive is part of G Suite and provides a user 30 GB of storage. You can purchase more if needed or as you add employees and switch to an enterprise account, you get additional storage for free.

Amazon

You can use Amazon Web Services and contract disk space and server space. This is not for the intermediate user, as it requires knowing how-to. While Amazon has great services, they don't make it the most intuitive process for the user.

Box

Box does still offer a free account, as of this writing, for 10 GB of space. I put Box in the same category as Dropbox that it does have a purpose, but it is hard to justify using it when you can get free file storage with Google and Office365.

One Drive

One Drive is the file storage service provided by Microsoft. It is included in the subscription of Office365 and includes a base storage of one terabyte. This is a lot of storage for a single user, and you could essentially back up your PC to the cloud.

Simple Marketing

If your opinion is that you really don't need a website to connect with your customers, then you can just go with getting a domain name to have a professional email address hosted. While you may feel this way, most people that are looking for services or products start with research on the internet. You severely limit your capacity to gain new clients without the ability for them to learn about you when and where they want. Prior to making a purchase today, buyers do research on the internet and can get all the way through a buying decision before they reach out to potential suppliers. Not giving your prospects the opportunity to learn about limits your business growth.

There are several SAAS (Software as a Service) choices that give you a low monthly cost and include easy-to-set-up website templates and hosting of your website. The most common are Wix, Weebly, square space, and Go Daddy.

Most of these include a domain name as part of your initial purchase; they also provide simple email management or the ability to bundle email and G Suite with the offer.

Leadpages

Another option rather than a website is to use a service like leadpages. The purpose of lead pages is to help you build a landing page that converts a visitor into a prospect or customer. You may be familiar with these types of pages where you go to and in a long form (extended explanation), or short form (simple squeeze page) look to get your email address or you to make a purchase. This software as service company provides hundreds of templates designed to provide information and capture email addresses. While this is more of a marketing tool that will be discussed further in marketing section, you can use it to create a homepage that could act as your website. Read more in marketing to see. If using lead pages makes sense, then it may be a good alternative for your first website. You can do so without a hosting service or domain, as they host the pages, letting you create an infinite number of pages.

I use it to build all types of pages for marketing, for myself and clients and find it a very useful tool for testing out new ideas quickly without having to set up a full-blown website.

Hosting Services

Hosting services tend to subsidize the cost of a domain name to keep you as a customer. This is a very competitive market, so shop around and check out the various deals. I like using Bluehost or Fatcow for hosting services. I have at least one website at each, so look at both and see who is currently offering the best deal, as the offers often change, given how competitive the hosting market is. Hosting provides you with a wide range of services from file storage, FTP, VPN, to simple website hosting where your files will reside and be served to visitors. Once you select a hosting service, you need to decide on a website system like WordPress. There are others, but none have the extensive plugins and complementary software that WordPress has.

First, a word of caution: if you are going to use WordPress, you want to use a host other than WordPress—a host like Bluehost or Fatcow.

At first look, wordpress.org looks to be an interesting option since they provide free websites and low-cost solutions for simple website hosting. If you are considering a WordPress site for free hosted by WordPress, you will need to understand the following two key points:

Free sites come with terms of service that WordPress can place advertising on your website. This means as you create content that draws customers, there could be advertisements on the site that offer competitive solutions.

The paid options remove advertising but have two inherent issues. The first is that the plugins available are limited; while this may not be an issue for simple sites, you limit your options to use some great tools that have been built for WordPress. Secondly, you cannot use tools like AdSense to serve ads to your website. While you may not want your website cluttered with ads to detract from your main message, if you were considering generating income from ad placement, then you need to have full control over advertising, and wordpress.org has limited the use of ad placement.

The true power of WordPress comes from the flexibility and customization and third party plug-ins. You can build a highly-customized site capable of just about anything with WordPress and a private host (including E-commerce). There really is no limit to what WordPress allows you to build and customize with a variety of special features and hooks to other programs. I use WordPress on a third-party host and feel it gives me the most flexibility.

Building a WordPress site requires extra work once you go beyond a simple theme template. You may need to hire someone to do a custom buildout if you don't have the time and skill set and require something beyond a homepage and blog.

MARKETING

I AM NOT sure who originated this simple explanation, but it wasn't me. This marketing analogy clarifies the parts that make up a marketing plan.

You own a Circus, and you arrive at a new town.

If you paint a sign and hang it up that says "Circus in town; come to the show tonight," that is **Advertising.**

If you put the sign on the side of an elephant and walk him through town, that is **Promotion.**

If you purposely walk by the elementary school, that is **Segmentation.**

If the elephant walks through the mayor's yard and crushes his flowers, and it makes the news, that's **publicity**

If you get the Mayor to laugh about it, that's **public relations.**

The town's residents come to the circus, and you tell them about the show, and how much fun they will have versus another activity, and they spend money on a ticket, that's **sales.**

If you created a plan and managed all these activities, that's **Marketing**!

LEAD GENERATION

What does Selling insurance, doing a Kickstarter campaign, or launching a book have in common? In all the cases, you need to identify people you can help, and then get them to take the time to learn about how you can solve their problem. The process usually starts out with leads or potential prospects that you can help. In some cases, you need to talk to that lead face-to-face or on the phone to qualify them and close them, but there is one significant change in the internet age. Customers tend to self-educate, and by the time they act, they have gone through 60% of the education process.

Having a process where you help a client to identify you as a potential solution to the problem they have, and they choose to either contact you immediately or go through a process of self-education prior to action is what has, in the past, been called a sales funnel. A conversion/sales funnel is somewhat an archaic idea because the metaphor is that you funnel down to the hot ready to close prospects and all other falls away. What you need to develop is a lead nurturing system, an automated process that guides prospects to the information they need to decide and qualifies them for your sales process and those that are less interested are not eliminated but rather can hang around you periodically check in with them to see if their need to buy has changed. This is what is known as a passive inbound lead nurturing system. To make your lead nurturing system even more powerful, you should think about how it appears to your potential audience and design it so that it can address a much wider group of prospects by how it messages.

The more you can be a trusted educator during this passive inbound process, the higher the chance the customer will select you for solving the problem or fulfilling their desire.

Let's go through an example of how a wider net can be cast for customers.

Let's say you're running a yoga studio. Just like Barnham & Bailey, you decided to get out of the circus business.

Your knowledgeable prospect is a person that practices yoga They know about you, your competitors, what they want, and you likely know how to engage with them because they are an obvious target customer. They will focus on your instructors, space, your hours, very specific yoga related issues, but speaking of those benefits to non-yoga people is just uninteresting noise.

Next are the Afflicted. These are prospects that have a problem but don't know that there is a solution for it. They certainly don't know you have the answer. An example is, someone that has back pain may not know that yoga is a solution for back pain. They also may have preconceived notions about yoga and wouldn't consider it as an option to solve back pain. Rather than positioning your yoga studio as a solution for back pain, you can present research about how stretching routines help to reduce inflammation and back pain. Those interested can then be educated as to how yoga is a stretching method with proven results. Opening the solution to the wider problem presents a much larger audience, but this audience will require education to get comfortable with the idea and then act.

The outer ring of potential leads are the oblivious. They may not fully understand how they can benefit from yoga as a stress reducer. Reaching out to people by asking questions relating to the effects of stress on their life can engage them to learn more. With a lead nurturing system that focuses on education—a lead that active meditation reduces stress and, along with it, high blood pressure, and promotes weight loss—you can cast an even wider net than just people who like to do yoga.

Each audience needs a different messaging and education process, and likely a different method of intervention.

Lead Nurturing typically begins with lead capture. You will need to interrupt a prospect and give them a reason to enter your system to learn more and eventually, when they are comfortable, to engage with you. The most common way on the internet is to use what is called a **lead magnet.** This is a report, list, system, or an ebook that provides help for free. The best ones come from a place where the content really does have value and benefit, not one of those lists you find on the internet that is just a tease to get you to buy something. Why, because you are looking to build trust and authority. If you want to be a gimmicky con man, then, of course, look for marks and run your scam, but if you believe in what you're doing and have a real solution, then come from a place of abundance and give something that can help. Prospects will see you as genuine and use your offer as a proof point to dig deeper into the content you provide about your solution and start to sell themselves.

In the case of our yoga studio, I would suggest three different lead magnets focused at the educated, the afflicted, and the oblivious—all with very different messages about how you can help. The prospect then self-selects by choosing a lead magnet and then, as you will learn later in email marketing, you can use this signal to tailor the conversation and education to the prospect.

Our Oblivious need time to learn that they have the problems, and then that there is a solution. In our yoga example, that may be an education series outlining spine health and back muscle conditioning and how poor back care creates low energy and mild to severe back pain; this could include some exercise challenges to confirm that yoga could be a solution. All free.

Next would be the afflicted; these are people that have identified they suffer from back pain either because they knew this or they have gone through the oblivious series. For this series, you can, again, provide education that helps the client to overcome some of the common objections to yoga and help them to see how it can solve their problem. In this series, you would have direct calls to action such as coming in for a free week of classes.

For the educated, you may have a completely different series focusing on your facility, instructors, and the nuances of the different types of yoga you provide. Again, leading to them having a clear call to action that gets them into the studio.

The passive system allows for the client to come to you when they are ready. When they are not and are preparing, you have little interaction. When they are ready, you make it easy for them to get your attention. Think about how much better this system works versus a list of leads you actively pursue.

In the passive system, we:

Automatically attract prospects with a "lead magnet"

We nurture them initially passively but provide methods for them to educate and warm up on their schedule

We only actively engage those clients that have asked for engagement so when you do have active contact, it is a very warm and interested prospect

Active System:

We assume all leads are at the same readiness to buy

We actively look to educate on our schedule

We don't have a system to allow self-nurture

A great way for someone to get your attention is to have a scheduling software like <u>Acuity Scheduling</u>. With this, they can set an appointment with you within a timeframe you have predetermined such as blocking out two mornings a week to take assessment calls. When clients are ready, then they can easily get 20–30 minutes of your time to talk about their needs. This is the essence of an inbound passive content system; you educate and help clients to assess your solution. When they are ready, they can get your attention, and then neither of you wastes each other's time because they are ready, and you can quickly assess if they are a good fit.

One of the best ways today to interact is through email. If your system provides this lead magnet—and for them to get it, they need to give you an email address to have you send the information—you have established an excellent introductory method of communicating with the prospect. From a technical aspect, this is very easy to do with the software I mentioned called <u>Lead Pages</u>. Even before you have a business, you can set up a landing page describing what you offer and get people to give you an email for your lead magnet. Next, we will cover how to best use emails in a passive marketing system that is not cheesy or sales.

EMAIL MARKETING

Email Marketing is still very powerful and, with the proper tools, provide you with an automated system for capturing and nurturing leads. Let's start with lead capture.

Your business will need an Email Service Provider (ESP) to manage your mailing list. I suggest two services; both are free, to begin with, and have pros and cons.

MailChimp is free up to 2000 users. It is the most widely used ESP and has the most integrations with other software. If you are using a website host like six or Go Daddy, there is an easy integration to capture emails and then put them into MailChimp. Both ESPs are free to low cost and don't require expensive expertise to set up. There are more sophisticated platforms that are complete marketing solutions, but they are expensive to start and maintain. I want you to have tools that are as close to free and let you test your ideas and let you scale up. You can always switch to a comprehensive platform if your business needs it and can afford it.

MailChimp is also working closely with two powerhouses: Facebook and Shopify. This means you can use your MailChimp to manage ads on Facebook as well as set up email automation to support your e-commerce. The integrations are easy to set up, and the automation is also simple to configure. There is not a lot of flexibility with the automation like there is in something like drip, but the reality is, most people would rather quick and easy set-up of a select set of automations than infinite flexibility.

Drip is free for the first 100 users and is different in that it is a tag driven versus list driven ESP. It comes with highly configurable automation and lends its self well to the construction of customer segmentation and multiple campaigns. It does not have the same drag and drop mail design as mail chip or constant contact.

I usually start new clients on MailChimp, as it is easier for them to work in to build newsletters.

Lead Pages

Earlier, we discussed lead capture via lead pages. If you use it or a software like it, you will need to integrate.

Make sure the Email capture form & pop up are not too distracting otherwise prospects will get annoyed with your efforts to get the email.

EMAIL MARKETING STRATEGY

If you just capture emails and then send out a monthly newsletter, you hate money. What I mean by this is, a person giving you that email is a signal that they have some interest in what you do; if it is just signing up for your newsletter or a lead magnet you have created to attract customers, you need to have a system for automatically nurturing the prospect towards a decision about your services.

E-mail Capture

Your website should have a Newsletter sign up. Even if you only plan to do a quarterly letter, you need to can capture an email address for those interested in your services. Basically, your newsletter is a generic lead magnet.

You should have a welcome/indoctrination series of emails for any new sign up. It can be as simple as one email that goes out automatically after sign up (this can easily be set up in an ESP). The welcome e-mail offers two things immediately to the person that signed up:

1. Some unexpected relevant information. Give them an option for a

lead magnet, report, hack list, or email mini course that you have created. They won't expect it, and you will see if they download or join, they are more active and need further engagement.

2. Ask them if they need help or have any questions and make it clear that if they email, you (or someone) will read the message and get back to them. In the end, you want to make a 1:1 connection, so always keep that door open to your prospect. The question they have could be the short path to a new relationship.

Once this is set up, it will work automatically and costs you nothing.

Capturing Email via Lead magnets

To effectively do a lead capture using a lead magnet, we need to:

1. Have an email service provider
2. Have a lead magnet
3. Be able to capture a lead and then serve up the lead magnet

You can do all of this in MailChimp, or you can combine it with your website or a tool like Leadpages. You would use lead pages or a web page as a landing page to describe why the lead magnet may be of interest. But you can just as easily have a link on your web page or embed a form from MailChimp into your homepage to capture the email.

Lead magnet

Your lead magnet needs to provide meaningful content but also must be brief. The offer needs to engage a prospect enough to give their email but not be too overwhelming. You will have much better luck with a one-page checklist or quiz to get initial interest and whet the prospect's appetite. You can then provide further content like an email mini course to educate. Spreadsheets, tools, and checklists or free e-books work well for lead magnets. To begin building my list for this book, I created a free ebook that covered the material about incorporation.

Next comes serving up the lead magnet. You need to create your follow-up email that includes a link to the file. In mail chimp (and the others), you can select the hyperlink tool and then select file instead of web. You will then be prompted to upload the file to the server. Now when the prospect gets the email, they can click on the link and get the magnet.

Exit and timed pop-ups. Having a pop up on page exit can be an effective way to capture emails. Leadpages includes leadboxes that can be timed or exit pop up for lead capture on your website. Take care not to have too many of these features on your website if there are timed pop ups as well as sign up bars it can get visually unpleasing quickly.

Automation

Using your email service provider to drip out content to help with client nurturing can be powerful. It does require you to think through the process and sometimes reverse engineer the process. The old Steven Covey line "begin with the end in mind" is poignant.

In our example, we want to bring someone from oblivious to making a buying decision. For the yoga studio, that means getting them to come into the studio, but you could be making an appointment for a call.

We need to think about what a prospect needs to know to make an informed decision, create that content, provide it in a way that is easy for them to consume; then, and only then, have our sales-based call to action. Through this process, if we plan it properly, we can use tools to help our prospect do the following:

Self-select so we can customize the content

Self-determine the speed they want to consume

Allow them to consume when and where they want. I found that the email mini course is a great way to provide this type of content.

Educate with the Email Mini Course

I think one of the best ways you can passively engage a client and learn about them is using email mini courses. Most ESPs have templates. Here is an example for you that shows how they work and how to use them. It is a short multiple email mini course on mini courses.

How to set up an email mini course

Why do I like them? They are easy to set up, and they are not too intrusive to the prospect. They can sign up and get them over days or weeks and either actively engage or, if they get busy with something else, come back to them. You can put in links and activities that segment and tag (depending on the ESP) to send the prospect better content. As you get more comfortable with automation and analytics, you can build powerful systems that engage and retarget the prospect on multiple platforms.

You can include video files links to worksheets and have links to progressive stages of education or segmentation to help you and the prospect figure out what they need to know.

E-mails with your E-commerce

I will go deeper into E-commerce later, but it is worthwhile to discuss how you can use emails to support your selling of product on the web. These can either be facilitated by the e-commerce platform or through connecting your ESP to the e-commerce system. Why would we connect them? Having the data from your e-commerce system transmitted to your ESP allows for you to use data to send out a relevant email. Below are some ideas of marketing automation you can implement; many of these are templates you can just activate.

Abandoned Cart

Every e-commerce site experiences users abandoning a cart. Around 50% of all transactions get dropped; it can be caused by technical reasons as well as user issues. No matter what the reason, following up automatically with an email can capture some of those sales.

Welcome Series after first purchase

Having a series of emails to welcome a new buyer to your community and to check in to make sure that the order and delivery went smooth will help to connect with the customer. I also suggest a second follow-up email to check in with the customer and request a review of the product and service. Social proof is a great lubricant for future sales, and it does not hurt to ask for a review. We all love it when we can use others' reviews to evaluate a purchase and getting reviews helps to build your community.

Win Back

Having an automated series that reaches out to customers and re-engages them with offers and coupons to get them to buy again can also boost sales. I usually set up a series of emails that go out 60, 90, 180, and 360 days after purchase that progressively increases discounted coupons. This is to get customers to come back and repurchase. Using email to automate this process has great ROI.

Remarketing

Shopify and MailChimp provide a method to retarget your customers with an email based on the products they have looked at on your site. There is also another ESP with an E-commerce focus called Klavyio that connects with E-commerce and automatically creates the emails to retarget your customer. You may have experience retargeting when you have been on a website looking at something, then every other website you go to has advertising for that exact product. This is retargeting advertising, but the next level is to retarget via email for those customers that you have email addresses.

High-value customers

Automatically reward your best customers. Using automation, you can trigger spend values that then send out coupons and deals to reward your best customers. Automating this process makes sure it gets done and done immediately

While email may someday be supplanted, it has held up the test of time. Understanding how to use this method of communication effectively as part of your marketing will accelerate your business growth and scale with your business without added resources or day-to-day handling by you or your team.

ChatBots

A new tool for customer interaction is the chatbot. Before I get into what a chatbot is, let's talk about why they are important.

How do you currently communicate with your loved ones?

Phone and text are the top two mediums with equal use.

Next question, do you still have a landline in your house?

Where am I going with this? Simple, most folks are only reachable now on a mobile phone and 50% of the time they are using a text messenger service. If your customers are messenger users then one way to connect is via text chat. The problem is people expect quick response so how do you do that?

This is where chatbots come into play. A chatbot provides an automated system for responding via messenger services. You can use it to answer common questions or run sequences just like an email campaign.

How would you use something like manychat? I think the best way is to answer frequently asked questions for your customers. You can have a menu with a tree to answer questions about returns, store hours, etc.

You can also automate customer service such as sending receipts, delivery information and follow up questions.

The real power of the message bot is it is immediate. Text messages have a 90% read rate and are read within five minute on average.

Added benefits with using Facebook messenger is that the user signs up instantly with the Facebook log in, you know the connection is legit not a made up email.

Below is a link to a chatbot sequence if you're a Facebook user. Give it a try and see how the automated bot provides you information in a quick conversational way.

ManyChat Link

I would be careful and respect the chat channel. If you start blasting it with deals and empty content you will be met with a wave of unsubscribes and lose this powerful connection with clients

Social Media

Social Media can be overwhelming. What platforms should you be using? How much time should you spend on them? What do you need to do to get results? And then every week there is a new platform or some new feature you need to learn.

Here is some guidance:

Look at the audience that the media can connect you to. If the audience is wrong, then the platform is wrong. Go where your customers are. If your customers are on Instagram, then work that platform. If they are on LinkedIn, then make that your primary platform. I will say given the tools provided and the size of the user base, it is hard to not participate on Facebook. More on them later.

Pick one or two and learn them well. You will have trouble keeping up with too many and then do them all poorly. If you're not sure, then start with Facebook. In this chapter, I will show you tools on how to use Facebook to connect with your customer.

Pick platforms that matter for your business to connect and communicate with potential customers. Understand how you're going to use the social media as a feature to establish authority, build a community, or acquire customers. If you're not doing one of the three, then it is a distraction; you can't pay bills with Facebook likes.

Facebook

Facebook is for everyone, and even with a business that may be B2B focused, you can use this platform to connect with clients. What makes Facebook so powerful is the data that it has on people and what they share coupled with Facebook's advertising infrastructure. If you are a consumer-facing business, Facebook levels the playing field by giving you cost effective means for connecting with your ideal client. So, how do you go about using Facebook to help your business or launch a book or product?

Facebook Page

Begin with a Facebook page

From your personal profile, you can create a business page for your venture. You will need this to anchor your pixel, advertising, and groups you may create.

Facebook Pixel

This is a non-negotiable item. If you are going to have an online presence, you need to create a Facebook pixel and integrate it into your marketing system.

The pixel is a piece of code that you can place on pages and into programs to track actions. This can get a little scary, but the fact is the fact. Not only does Facebook have all this data on who are your friends, what movies you like, and anything else you share on Facebook, but they associate your movements on the internet with your profile. There are millions of these pixels all over the internet, and they are collecting every page you look at every click and then using this to fuel the data engines for advertising.

Once turned on and placed on your website pages and in various other tools, you will be able to track who visits your site and does various activities. You may have been subject to this where you have done something outside of Facebook yet when you in Facebook, you now get ads related to the site you visited. This is called retargeting, and it's one of the tools available to you.

Even without a pixel in place on your website (let's say you don't have one yet), you can begin to use Facebooks advertising features. Here is one starter idea: many people struggle with building an email list. They can set up MailChimp, create a lead magnet, but then they say, "How do I get traffic to my sign up?" If you are prepared to pay $5 a day, you can begin to drive very targeted traffic to your list. In fact, you can make a direct connection between Facebook and MailChimp so the prospect never must get out of the Facebook platform.

Let's look at two examples. First, our yoga studio and second, an author looking to build a list for a book launch.

In the case of the yoga studio, we can search by geography and select people close to the studio because we know that location is a major factor; we could target age and gender to be more specific, but then we can target interests, specifically yoga, finding people that would be good for creating a lead generation campaign for our educated audience, but what about the afflicted? I did a search on my hometown in audience insights for people with interest in back pain, and Facebook said there was 0-500 active monthly users, mainly women over the age of 65. So, we could do a targeted lead magnet on five things you can do now to relieve back pain and increase mobility and develop a campaign through email that focuses on older women and getting them into an intro yoga program.

For an author, you can use the same method of creating a lead generation campaign, but now, you do a nationwide search for ebook readers that like an author that is like what you write. If you give away a short story or novella, you can attract readers to your list. The nice thing is, you can start this for as low as $5 a day, and you can turn the ad on and off instantly.

Why should you take a broader approach and place the pixel to track visitors to your website, a specific page, or for a specific action? The data from website visits and other interactions can be used to either find more people like those that are interested in you products, or we can target those visitors with better messaging.

On a recent campaign I ran for the launch of a book, we did a Facebook live which the author posted, introducing the book and offering a launch promotion. We then sent it out to a cold audience designed to target customers with interest in fashion. The ad did well, but this was just our first iteration.

After running the ads for a few days, we created a lookalike audience of people who watched the video more than 75%. The video was about one minute, so for folks to watch it that far on Facebook meant they were really interested. When we switched to that group, our conversion rate doubled!

Later, when we had enough traffic to the author's website (about 500 visits), we were then able to create a lookalike audience of those people and increase conversions by another 50%.

Facebook Live

Using live video on Facebook is a great way to promote your business. The problem most entrepreneurs have is, they are camera shy, and that gets in the way of using a powerful free tool. Facebook, YouTube, Netflix, and Amazon are all executing strategies to establish dominance in video in the 21st century. Facebook seeks a place where platform users for content generate content and to establish dominance in this space they are actively promoting live video—meaning you will get further reach, engagement and priority placement in your friends and followers feeds when you use it.

For local businesses, live should be thought of as free commercials. In the past, you likely did not run commercials because of the production cost and air time and for most, these costs are still too high; furthermore, you never had any insight into what the ad spend was delivering, but through the pixel system, you can access the data and use it to further hone your message and nurture your clients. Use it for flash sales and updates and self-directed promotion, even if no one joins your live when you produce it, you will get a following post live broadcast.

Groups

If you are trying to build a community using Facebook, groups can be the tool to use. I suggest thinking about setting up the group so it is of benefit to the users, not you. Too many groups I see are all about the facilitator using a channel rather than like-minded people connecting around what you do.

Advertising on Facebook

Facebook is an advertising platform; that's how they make money. It allows the individual and small business to be competitive and economical in their advertising, but it's not easy. Facebook makes changes about every quarter and adopts new tools and strategies. It can be like the wild west. If you dig into it, you can be a leader in your space, but it will take time and learning to stay ahead on the curve.

Instagram

Instagram is part of Facebook and is slowly adopting Facebook's advertising and analytics platform. While I am not a big user, I have seen clients that have had good results.

Certain products lend themselves well to Instagram—visual products, beauty, and fashion—mainly business to consumer. If you can build an audience on Instagram, then you can get a very loyal low-cost connection with a community. I would work to get them actively connected via Facebook.

You can build up your audience by following a process of going and liking similar feeds. Those you like tend to follow you back, and if you actively work this, you can quickly build a following.

You should switch your Instagram from personal to business and attach it to your Facebook page for continuity and to get analytics on who is visiting your Instagram.

Influencers

Working with influencers

Marii (pronounced like Mary) Lang is a business owner that created a product to clean makeup brushes. Like most businesses, it started from what Marri saw as a hole in the market. Her product has been solely promoted on Instagram at this writing; with less than two years under her belt, she has been able to quit her day job, and through her sixteen thousand direct followers and co-branding with other influencers, she has been able to grow her brand. Swirl and Sparkle does not do any traditional marketing or even use email lists. To me, this proves if you're committed to a platform, you can make it work for you.

If you are going to work with influencers on Instagram or YouTube, be sure you understand the reach and impact they can deliver and that you can do a clear ROI calculation. Many influencers cannot demonstrate direct sales results for companies, and that is fine if you're giving them some product samples, but if they are charging for promotion, get proof of results.

Twitter

I run a Twitter account, and over time, I have built up several thousand followers. Here, again, if you can see a direct correlation between the platform and your customer, get after it. My experience is, Twitter just helps me amplify content to others, and I have recently started to use it only to put out original content and have reduced the number of tweets to a few per week. As an advertising platform, if my trials were not positive and given how difficult the platform is for advertising, I will not put any money into it until I see substantial changes.

Search

I have spent the first part of the chapter covering social media, but there is an equally important internet marketing tool—and that is search. The top three search engines are Google, YouTube, and Amazon. Optimizing your content for search engines is very important and ever-changing. Don't get obsessive with SEO; rather, develop substantial solid content for your passive marketing and Google and lesser search engines will index it properly.

If video is relevant content for you, hosting it on YouTube and developing a YouTube channel is helpful. YouTube is quickly becoming the number one place to get how-to information. YouTube can be a great promotional resource for your business; if you have an expertise, you can show off your authority.

Google Advertising has two parts to consider. The first is traditional search and getting your ad placed in advance of search results. This can be expensive, and in highly competitive search terms, the bids are high. To put it into perspective, a suggested bid for a keyword search on "Should I Incorporate?" runs $8–20. I can target a click on Facebook of $3. The second use of Google is retargeting visitors of your website with ads on other websites. Google has the largest retargeting advertising market. Using Google retargeting is getting easier, and now with the competition they face from Facebook, they are providing more resources to help individuals get ads placed. If you are going to pursue this as an advertising platform, you will need to spend some serious time learning or hire someone.

SALES

BRICK AND MORTAR retail sales have really struggled in the last few years; this is not because people are buying less but buying differently. The habit changes to be more comfortable with online purchases and the trend towards mobile means you need to have a multi-pronged approach to sales. If you are a small local retailer, you are in a better place than you might think if you can strike the right balance between having a physical store and developing an online presence. Not that you have plans for world dominance (you may look where Sam Walton started) but, more so, to serve your local customers that are not likely to come into the store as much.

E-Commerce

If you are going to be selling products online, then consider a solution that has built-in e-commerce, like Shopify. The other website providers I noted above also offer e-commerce solutions; however, I would characterize the other website as generalists versus being an E-commerce specialist. Shopify makes it easy for you to sell on Facebook, Pinterest, and other platforms with minimal additional set up. You can purchase domains through them or set up a store without a domain under the myShopify domain.

Shopify provides simple free website templates or the ability to buy specialized templates to set up a theme for your site. The real strength comes from the integrated e-commerce that links to social media channels to market and sell your products all for a set monthly fee and a processing fee that is like those of other credit card processors. For an additional fee, you can add a point of sale equipment for a bricks and mortar store.

If E-commerce is a significant part of your online presence, then this can also act as your website. The other option for e-commerce that works well with WordPress is WooCommerce. It allows for more customization and has fixed upfront costs for setting up rather than on-going monthly fees, but it now requires you to stay on top of updates that Shopify includes as a service.

Both are good, and I have been involved in large installs of both and conclude that if you are going to be highly customized, Woo is a better choice. If you're looking for an easy-to-run system that is robust, go with Shopify. I also like how Shopify, MailChimp, and Facebook play together and make it easy to put in some advanced marketing features like dynamic product retargeting and email automation.

Most blog sites like Wix and square space also include e-commerce functionality. These are not as robust as Shopify and WooCommece but can be used for light commerce.

Commerce Via Fulfillment Businesses

Today you can have a retail business from your home and never touch a product. The days of having your garage or spare room full of product and you're up until the wee hours packing boxes the running to the post office to ship are gone. You can use fulfillment companies to essentially outsource your entire operations, managing your inventory, pick, pack, ship, and deal with payment processing and returns.

The value you add is through funding the inventory and developing a marketing strategy for the products you sell. Yes, you will forfeit margin for all the services provided by the fulfillment company, but you also do not have to build out or support Best of all, you get to use companies like Amazon that are allowing you to use the cutting edge internal processes that they have. You also have the added benefit that they typically deal with all payment processing. You end up with three roles, the most important being a marketer of what you are selling; next is being a capital provider for the business, and, finally, you may create added value through arbitrage of product sourcing. The single biggest system for this type of operation is fulfillment by Amazon. You can run your entire business off their platform selling side by side with Amazon and thousands of other sellers. This is a growing cottage industry where sellers locate and market products overseas for sale. There are also tools like Yasiv and unicorn smasher to help you to identify products to sell. Beware: there are lots, of course, promoting the idea how you can make millions selling on Amazon with little work. While the work and logistics are limited because of the use of fulfillment, it is a dynamic and competitive business. In many categories, you are competing with other fulfillers as well as Amazon.

Another way to include sales on your site without necessarily running a full fulfillment business is using Amazon affiliate links to promote products. If there is a range of product or supplies that compliment your service and you want to make it easy for your client to source them on your site, you can do so with the affiliate program and earn 2-12% on a range of products and services.

Measuring and Reporting

The number of items that can be measured in a business is endless and can become a full-time job preparing an analysis data. I would like to give you a few introductory tools to help you determine your business performance. While I will be talking about these as they relate to sales, the tools can be applied to any metric of the business to give you better insight.

Using trailing twelve-month averages provides you with a way to look at your business performance without seasonality and help you to identify long-term performance. Using month-to-month charts for performance analysis can be tough when your business has seasonality or chunky sales. By applying an average, we smooth this out and can begin to identify and contrast trends. (Remember, you can access the worksheets at this link for trailing twelve-month T12A, trailing three-month, and alternate charts of 52 and 13 weeks.) If you have a commerce business and are using basic reporting, sometimes the best thing to do is, make this part of your weekly reporting and grab the numbers from Shopify, Woo, or Amazon. Frankly, weekly gives you finer detail, and I feel it's better, but it does require weekly reporting.

Begin either with the 12-month or the 52-week and fill in historical data up through the current period.

You notice the worksheet automatically creates the three month/13-week average. Look at the data and think back to that past ups and downs of your business. I bet you can connect the past downturns with instances where the 3month/13-week indicator breaks below the 12/52 line and times of good growth align with when you have had the short-term indicator above and leading the 52-week line.

This becomes a key performance indicator for your business; keeping the shorter-term measurement of sales above the longer term is the simple goal. Every week, if you can just push up those sales, even if it is only a dollar, that keeps the short-term indicator above the longer term. When you see upsets to the short term, and it is trending three or four weeks down, you can react and address what is causing this downturn and correct before it becomes a larger long-term issue.

Trailing three-month and Twelve-month averages are great tools for evaluating any trends that you need to take out the noise and evaluate. I have used them to do analysis on oil price, inventories, all kinds of issues, to help to see that the short-term work is influencing the bigger picture in the right way.

The next charts are derivatives of the averages. What that means is, we are doing an analysis of the analysis. These ratios help you to see expansion (any number above 0) or contraction (any number below 0) week over week and year over year. Over time, these indicators of your velocity will help you to get a feel for the magnitude of change and help you to understand the severity of situations—both positive and negative.

How could growth be a problem? You now have a great visual indicator of your growth rate and keeping on the right growth rate keeps you within your ability to create and collect cash to increase working capital. If you see your 13-week lasting off at a new velocity, you can start to think through how you can best manage the upcoming working capital needs you may have.

This is by no means all the reporting tools available, but if you begin to use these indicators along with your 52-week cash flow and monthly financials, you have a comprehensive toolbox for finding and fixing business operational issues.

If you want to you these tools on other business metric great, I have run charts that track revenue and expenses to make sure they are staying in line as the business grows and, of course, expanding the charts as you go to include more than one year of data gives you a historical perspective.

Now to dive a little deeper into concepts around growing your business ...

Burn rate

This is a term for a planned negative cash flow usually associated with a startup or new initiative. It takes cash to make cash, and there are times where initial investment is required to get a strategy in place. Knowing the negative cash implications for your venture and the time that you expect to be running negative are critical. To figure this out, you will need to do a Break-even analysis.

Break even analysis

You can use our break-even analysis spreadsheet to analyze a specific project. If you are trying to do this for the entire business, then the work should be done via a business model or using the 52-week cash flow model. In a B/E analysis, you are looking to determine the number of units you need to sell in each period to be cash flow neutral. While cash flow neutrality still leaves you at the whim of your cash collection cycle, "treading water" means you can continue at that level and keep the doors open.

The next concept to understand is the Sale trough; understanding and planning for this phenomenon when you grow your business will keep you out of trouble. Many times, business owners are cautious when dealing with getting to breakeven, but when times are good, they don't plan the impact of growth. They figure it's all good because we got the orders coming in but poorly planning growth can cause trouble; that's why understanding how to navigate a sales trough is critical for solid hassle-free growth of sales.

The Sales Trough

The sales trough is the name for the phenomena that happens when you grow your sales and the sales associated costs to ramp up sales. Owners have had to struggle through a growth curve because of poor planning and, through the process, lost some of the momentum or potential customers because of not fully understanding this phenomenon. While some of this have been covered in working capital, I think it is important to dig deeper into what to expect as you grow your business and the potential pitfalls.

Entrepreneurs tend to be aggressive when presented with an opportunity to get new customers or increase sales. Fortune favors the bold. The theme here is not to be pessimistic about growth opportunities but rather to get you to be aware of why many companies get discouraged about the results of a new sales initiative. You will have far more success and retain your customers and good reputation if you think through some of the questions below and have answers for them. Setting the right growth rate and having a sustainable tempo is far better for your business momentum than fits and starts, as you have to compensate for your poor planning.

How much cash will you need to keep your customers happy with delivery times?

How much cash would you need to have if you were going to hire a new sales person?

What other costs increase with sales? Insurance, service support, etc.

How long will it take to get our cash back on the investment?

Let's look at material cost first. If you are planning a sales initiative that will increase sales, and you wish to keep your delivery times as they currently are, you will need to build up inventory, get consignment inventory, or work out some type of drop shipment from your vendors.

In getting ready for a growth initiative that is tied to a product sale, you need to look first: is this product-driven or customer-driven? A pure product-driven sales initiative means you know the product you will be selling. If, however, your sales initiative is focused on a customer segment that may be choosing from a range of your products, you will need to assess what this product will be. A good way to do this is to review similar customer sales and look at the following:

Rank product popularity: what sold the most?

Look at average sale size to understand quantity order

Evaluate product mix to assure you can meet the mix demand

This assessment will help you to have the right inventory in stock and to focus your dollars on the right inventory.

The next assessment must be on lead time for orders. If you are sourcing from overseas or selling complex or handmade product, you need to make sure that you have your inventory orders staged properly. This could mean that you need to stock up on finished goods and increase raw materials. Unless you have special terms, you will likely need to outlay this cash first and with this, so starts the outgoing cash flows that dig a hole in your working capital.

Seller Cost

Will you hire on a new seller for this growth and do they require salary and benefits? You also need to calculate and add your training costs, hiring costs and include payroll taxes that you're now obligated to pay. Sellers can be the single biggest hole digger if they do not start selling quickly.

Example of a sales trough

In the following example, we will hire a sales person for 25,000 base and them earning 10% commission with the expectation of earning 50,000 in year one. The Sales person has another $2,000 a month as expenses, including payroll taxes. The seller has a $250,000 annual quota. In month one, you order the extra stock you will need for what he will sell, and you have a month of no sales while the seller is onboarding.

You need another 80 units to cover the upcoming growth; however, your supplier only ships in a 100 count, so you now have the additional inventory count as well as the carry cost of the new inventory.

This example assumes we get somewhere between 45-60 days' credit on our order and that it takes our seller a few months to get to quota. The selling ramp up is no sales in the first month 50% of quota in month two and on quota from month three on. We collect from our clients in thirty days with commission being paid after collection. Below is a graph of how the trough develops.

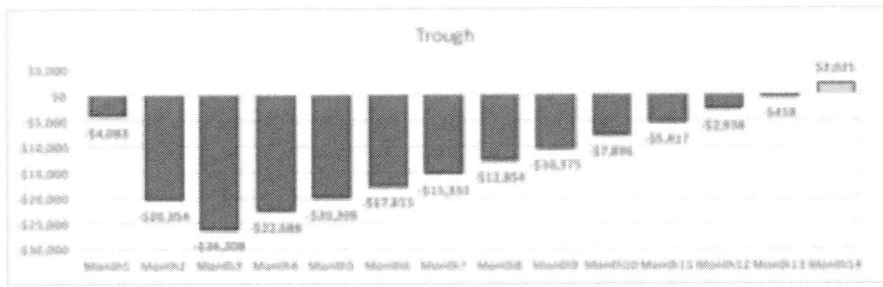

As you can see from this chart, there needs to be a cash reserve of $26,208 to cover the month three hole that is dug from the additional cash needs of inventory increases, salary increases, and the extension of credit to the new clients. It will take almost a year and a half to get back to where we started with cash, but at the end of two years, we will have $26,814 in cash collected, and that is an 18% IRR for the project.

The issue with sales troughs is: they can look good from a return perspective, but without proper analysis of how the opportunity will impact cash, you can get yourself into trouble quick. This is particularly the case when hiring sale people; they come with high costs. Many times, the full cost is not considered (payroll tax, benefits); if they don't work out, the trough goes deeper and to stop this high cost, you need to go through the pain of firing an employee.

Beyond the costs captured in the above example, there are some other costs that should be considered in the evaluation.

Material Cost

If you sell a product, you will likely have added carrying costs in inventory and handling. The offset is not to have the inventory then disappoint new customers with longer lead times. If your sellers don't move product, then these costs mount unless your vendors are prepared to provide material on consignment, drop ship, or give you extended terms.

Support Cost

Will you need to upgrade support systems along with the growth to keep your customers happy? Support services tend to get lost in the growth plans and can result in either added costs or disappointed customers. Think through the customer experience and make sure that you have thought through those added costs and built them into your trough.

Insurance Cost

Here is one that can sneak up on you. If you are carrying general liability insurance for your business that is tied to your sales volume, then you might get a surprise at the end of the year. There is a clause in your insurance rider that says the insurance company audits your business and then adjusts your premiums based on sales volume. A great sales year can lead to a whopping insurance premium, so find out what your provider's ratio is so you can apply it to your planning if you are expecting a big pickup in sales.

For those with a plan to raise funds from others to fund stellar growth, having a detailed understanding of your sales trough is critical. You should do a sales trough analysis along with doing the advanced modeling techniques from financial modeling to determine the probabilities of hitting sales goal that you associate with new sellers.

There is a lot of risks associated with human capital and sales. In our example above, our seller started hitting quota within six weeks of being hired—an optimistic projection, given most sales organizations experience 20-30% attrition. If an organization brings a seller on the payroll, and he does not meet quota and then leaves, he does not take the hole in your cash with him.

INVENTORY AND PRICING

THEORETICAL: YOUR PRODUCTS AND OR SERVICES

YOU SOLVE problems or fulfill desires for your customers. You do this by providing a solution or a need/want. It can be a service you provide such as an accountant or it may be a physical or digital product that you sell at a physical or virtual location. No matter what your product or service is, you need to have a deep understanding of its flow and impact on your business and customer to maximize the profit you can extract from it.

I have evaluated numerous businesses to help them with operations. It may come as no surprise that while a company may have a high level of expertise about how a product can be of benefit to the user of the product, and the company generates sales from solving problems with said product, they have limited knowledge on the impact of that product within their own business.

The Pareto principle or 80/20 rule gets thrown around quite a bit, and here it comes again. I have found in multiple projects that around 80% of a business's revenue come from around 20% of its products, give or take a few percentage points. When working with F. H. Steinbart, the oldest homebrew store in the United States, 70% of the revenue came from 28% of the SKU (504 products). It is representative of other businesses I have dealt with as an operator or a consultant.

This ratio has significant implications for inventory, margins, revenues, and overall customer perception. If you can, get these products right to have a logarithmic effect on the businesses profitability and ability to serve its customers.

Furthermore, if you can, get the price, stock, and service right on the 20%.

PRACTICAL: YOUR PRODUCTS AND OR SERVICES

Begin by ranking your products or services based on annual sales. At the simplest level, just rank annual sales volume; however, it is helpful to also see the number of transactions to get that sales volume. The second variable helps to weight products on order size; we want to treat large one-off orders differently than smaller consistent orders. If you feel there are shifts from year to year, you can include more years to the analysis.

I typically export a detailed listing of the company SKUs or products to excel and create a table and then sort the rows in descending order in the annual sales column.

Annual sales volume, Number of orders, retail price, and average price as a minimum but I would suggest getting as big a data dump as possible.

ONE PRODUCT METHODOLOGY

Starting with the item (product or service) that accounts for the largest percentage of sales, do a deep dive on this product.

When a business has product/service issues that need to be addressed, I use the One Product Methodology. We audit the company offerings starting from the product that drives the most sales and work our way down the list. If you address one product a week, this way, you will typically touch 25% of sales on a business with around 2,000 SKUs. That's right; 52 products delivering 25% of the impact. This can be enlightening as to how much you really don't know about what makes you the most money. In the case of our home-brew supply, the number one product accounts for 3.3% of total sales and is on 60% of the orders they place. Screwing this up has a big effect on sales and a bigger effect on the number of customers it can impact.

Before we go deeper into analysis and examples, let's think about the physical location of the products. From an inventory standpoint, do you have these high-volume items in the right location?

Think about this from the logistics perspective of fulfillment by yourself or others. For example, this exercise influenced the clients' choice of where to place the product for inventory storage so on high volume days, the staff could restock quickly and where the products were in the store, locating high moving product so that it was convenient for clients to get to and drew them past other add-on items.

Here is an example of working through a set of these numbers:

Example:

Annual Sales 22,000

Quantity sold 20,000

Quantity of orders 1632

Retail Price $2.25

Average Price $2.20

Divide sold by orders to get average number sold per order.

Do you sell a lot of one offs or multiple units per order?

We now can understand some things about inventory:

Average order size is 13.48 items

Average orders per month 136

Average sales quantity per month 1,883

After evaluating the turnaround time on orders, we know that it takes about two weeks from order to receipt, so a reorder level is set 50% of 1,883 or 916; this gets us turnovers to maximize our inventory. To fully understand this cost, you must also know your inbound freight costs and your storage costs. This is particularly important when using an outside fulfillment provider where you will pay for shipping as well as have a cost for storage space.

Now we can look at our inventory levels and set stock reorder points to eliminate the dreaded stock out. Having minimum quantities that are tied to our analysis.

We can explore supply chain logistics and evaluate the price quantify breaks against inventory storage to establish our best costs. If we are shipping nationally, does it make sense to deploy the inventory to multiple locations to shorten customer delivery?

Monthly and seasonal analysis

Using some of our analysis tools, we can plot 12-month and three-month averages to see if there are seasonal shifts. If you look back and see a sinusoidal wave on the three-month, you likely have seasonality and can find some savings though adjusting stock levels through the year.

POCKET PRICE

This expertise entails you taking all the cost and applying them to a product. Starting with you supply cost and working through to the actual sale price, you can see what margin you pocket. Below is a list that covers most of the items you will need to account for, but you may have additional items or different ones for your products.

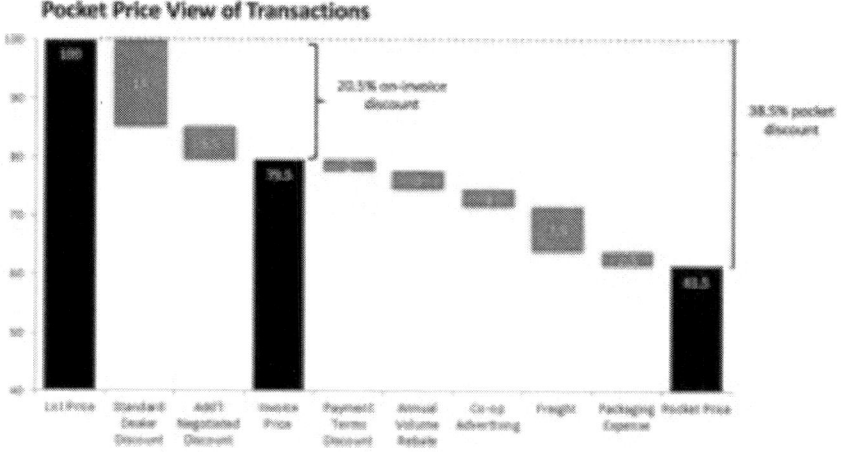

Product cost: What you actually pay for the product.

Payment discounts or purchase incentives: There may be payment discounts that you apply for cash payment or early payment.

Quantity rebates: There may be rebates based on your annual purchase that should be applied and are not on the invoice because they are handled as part of some promotion from your supplier.

Inbound freight: What does it cost you to get the product into your building? Does it cost the same all the time? Do you routinely rush product at a premium?

Fulfillment costs: If you are using a fulfillment service, what is the cost to store, pick, and pack?

Outbound freight: What is the freight cost? You should identify what it costs you to ship and then what you recover in shipping. Across your whole business, this is your freight recovery ratio, and in a perfect world, it is 100%, but if it is not, then this is a discount on the product that needs to be accounted for.

Discounts any deals or discounts that move a list price to an average price.

Quantity price breaks: Another type of discount can be quality breaks of volume incentive you give to customers.

When you go through this process, you will be surprised to find out that your true margins are not what your think. This will help you with determining the best list prices and discount structure going forward. I have done this for multiple businesses for literally millions of SKUs and found clients routinely selling some products at a negative margin, not as part of a strategy to gain market but plain old poor pricing practices.

If you feel your business has some real inventory issues, I would suggest an active approach and get you and your team on an analysis of the 20% that drives your 80% revenue; everyone finds issues and fixing this issue means they will go from being repeatedly negative transactions to repeatedly positive ones.

PRICE SENSITIVITY AND STRATEGIC PRICING

As a follow-up on inventory, pricing is a natural offshoot. Most companies don't have a pricing strategy or system. While they believe in ideas like higher volumes attract better discounts, there is little organization brought to how discounts are dispensed. When working at a pricing consultancy, we would help companies develop pricing systems. Initially, we would do an extensive statistical analysis of the existing pricing structures and from that, find out where we could help.

PRICING STRATEGIES FOR SERVICE

As a rule of thumb, if you're charging an hourly rate, three times the underlying cost will get you a workable number for charging.

At the end of each year, contact your clients that you will be increasing your prices by the consumer or producer price index. This is a reasonable increase and easily explainable, as you just keep your costs in line with the national average. The important part is, you and your clients get into the habit of this price increase.

You also offer to them the option to purchase as much of your time now at current prices for next year; this presents the price increase in a value-added way: "Prices are going up, but you can get a special deal and lock in last year's rates with booking time now." The funny thing about this price increase gambit is that many of my clients have adopted it and use it now if they sell hourly rate work. This works for graphic designers, developers, and plumbers.

Switching to solution selling and developing a solution-based approach is a great way to get out of selling hours. There are two good books: the 1988 classic SPIN Selling and Think like your customer. Both lay out selling processes that help you to identify what is important or painful to your customer and positioning what you do as the solution to that problem. With the tools that you have picked up in this book, you should be able to identify and quantify the cost of the problem to your client and then show the ROI on what you do. Let's use an example that I had with a client where I had a client that I could help with around one week's work that on an hourly rate would be around $7,200. Instead, I focused on solving a recurring $100,000 a year problem for only $25,000. Delivering a 400% ROI in year one!

Gainsharing—another pricing strategy that is results-focused. This only works with certain services and can lead to clients feeling you're making too much money. In our pricing business, we did our work on contingency getting 25% of the resulting margin lift we created. So, for every dollar we created, we got twenty-five cents.

We did end up spending extra time in the selling process establishing the baseline that the client was comfortable with, and we had a few situations where customers would rather be going with a flat rate, but the option of aligning your incentives with your client can make for a long lasting strong relationship.

Pricing Strategies for E-commerce and Distribution

What about companies that sell products? That is even easier. Businesses that sell a wide range of products to a diverse customer set have data within their historical sales that can be used to evaluate if they are pricing to maximize profits. I worked for several years in a pricing consultancy, and we did work with distributors and resellers to help them identify price optimization opportunities. In every instance, we found a low correlation between price and volume. As you see in the example below, you should have an expected fit of volume to discount awarded.

We would then apply strategies to improve margins through giving the company guidelines and systems to manage price. As you can see, just getting the customers that were priced too low to either get to the right price or stop selling to them would improve the businesses performance.

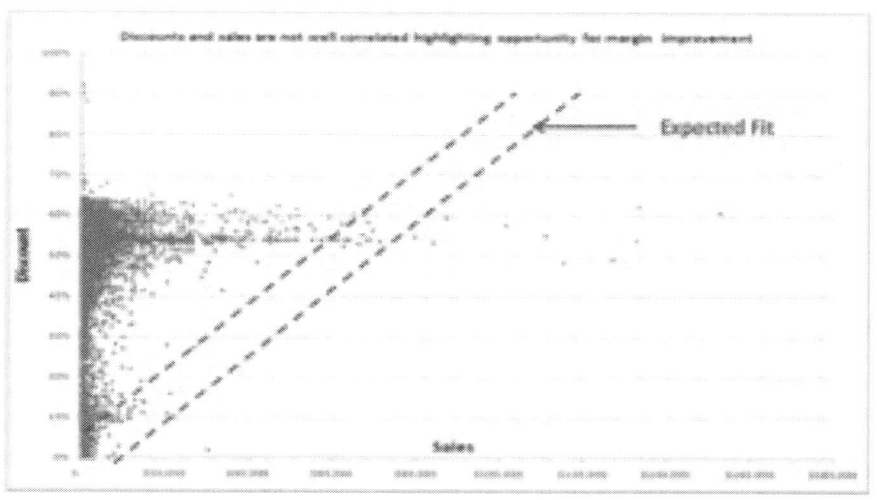

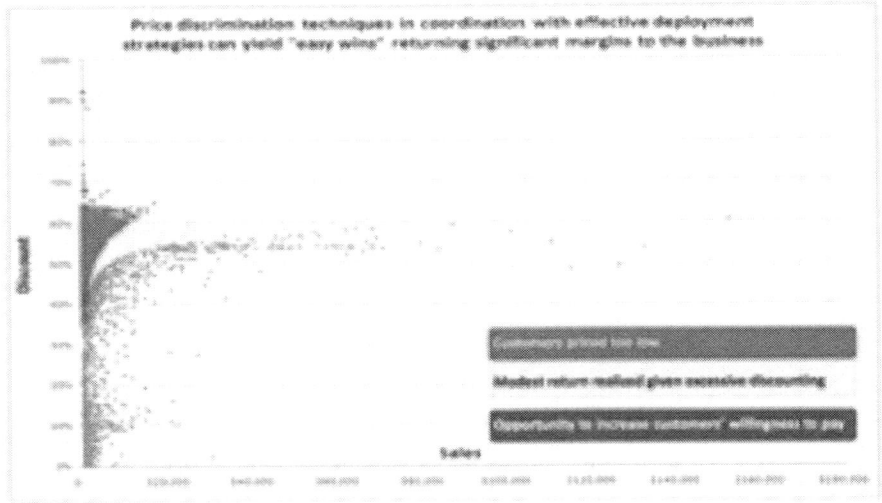

For our solution to work, you needed to be of a certain scale. We could deliver 3-5% margin

improvement in ninety days; the solution was complex, and we were paid a percentage of the lift we created. The reason I bring this up is not to sell you on hiring a pricing consultant but rather to share with you some of the foundational concepts that apply to all businesses and if you put in place some of these disciplines. You will have better than average margins. I will also help to dispel some of the common price and discount myths.

The dynamics of discounting

Let's say you sell a product for $10, and it has a 30% margin.

If you discount this product by 10%, how many products do you need to sell to make up what you're losing in the discount?

The answer is, you need to increase sales of that product by 50% to offset the lost margin.

Math

$10-$7 = $3 Margin Sell. Sell a unit =$3

10% discount

$10 -$1 = $9; $9-$7 =$2

$3/ $2 = 1.5

You should do this math to determine if it makes sense to do any discounting as a promotion.

Conversely, the owner is afraid of raising prices and the loss of business a price increase would cause. This assumption is false as most price increases never cause a big enough loss of business to offset what is made from the increase.

Let's say you sell $100,000 a year of sales with an average gross margin of 30% and decide to do a general price increase of 3%.

Math

100,000 x 30% = 30,000

Price increase 3%

$103,000 New GM = 33% = $33,000

You would have to lose 8.8% of sales ($9,090) to offset the bottom line improvement from the price action. Let's say you have highly sensitive customers and lose 4% of your sales; you still benefit by 1.5% increase in revenue with fewer sales.

That is the power of pricing.

What if you had a way to get a 3-4% price increase while still giving your customer the perception of being the value player?

Let's begin with the psychology of pricing and why a thoughtful, disciplined price strategy is important for your business.

The exact numbers for your business will be slightly different, and by going through the inventory exercises, you will know exactly the ratios but based on the 80/20 rule, 80% of your revenues come from 20%, and those are the products your customers are most sensitive to your price in comparison to your competitors. These are the things that they buy almost every order, and the cost of the product directly impacts them, likely as a cost of doing business. By identifying these products and then setting the prices competitively, we take advantage of the psychology that your client will assume that all your prices are of the same perceived value. From your customer's perspective, when they evaluate your price, they see the inverse—meaning their perception is that 80% of what they buy from you is priced competitively. The other 20% will not have the same physiological weight that the sensitive items have; it's either the client won't question the pricing because they just are not familiar or if they do, you have a reasonable explanation in that these items are slower moving items that you carry as a convenience to your client and if they were to buy more, you could have similar pricing levels.

My analogy is milk and toothpicks. People are conscious of the price of milk or eggs, items they buy with frequency, and they choose where to purchase based on the price of the milk. While at the store buying milk, if you need toothpicks, you just pick them up; you don't think too much about the price, as that boy will last you a few years. So, what the smart stores do is set a price that draws you in for the milk but then set a higher margin on the toothpicks because they are a low sensitivity convenience purchase. We need to determine what is your milk and toothpicks.

The products your customer is sensitive to are those that make up the largest portion of your sales. The twenty percent that constitute 80% of revenue. We already have a good idea of the products based on doing the inventory evaluation.

Here is a simple exercise: Begin with the products that create 80% of your sales; this should end up constituting 20-25% of your SKU count. These are your sensitive items. Next, look at the rest of your sales and identify the next 10% of sales; these constitute low sensitivity items. Then look at the SKUS that make up the last 10% of sales; these are your insensitive items.

Now, at the end of the year, rather than raise all prices by the same amount, follow this process:

Find out from suppliers if there will be any price increases that you will be getting from them and then apply the cost increases you will be getting. You need to pass this along; otherwise, you will suffer from margin erosion over time on top of these costs, and they will likely be different for every product or supplier; you need to apply a general price increase.

To figure out what to increase prices, we use a table like the one below:

We take last year's sales and make the volume cuts of 80/10/10. Then we apply a staggered price increase, having the lowest on the sensitive items and then moving up. This table, when you finish putting in your margin increases by the three sensitivity categories, shows you the total increased margin of $17,103 and the blended price increase of 3.015%.

	Increase	1.75%	6.65%	9.50%
	$ Volume	80%	10%	10%
Total Sales	$567,252	$453,802	$56,725	$56,725
Projected Total	$584,355	$461,743	$60,497	$62,114
Increased Margin	$17,103			
Price Increase	3.015%			

If you are still concerned about increasing prices, try this out at the end of the year but just use small numbers to test it out. Then if you see no pushback from customers, then mid-year, double the increase in the low sensitivity and insensitive items.

Now, what is the justification for the extra costs tied to the low and no sensitivity items? This is an easy story; these are items that you carry to support your customer that are slow moving and higher cost for you to support; therefore, as a one stop shop, you need to capture that value.

What about product mix differences in your customer base? This is where real-time statistical analysis can really shine, but for small operators, doing this on your own, you need a simple solution. Rather than have a one size fits all discounting structure, you need to lock it to volume. The next best solution is to do the same 80/20 analysis by customer and use this evaluation to see if any of their sensitive items are coming from a low or no sensitivity category. If they are, you can do special discounting for that customer.

PLANNING AND TIME MANAGEMENT

PLANNING

AS I DID research for this book and interviewed business owners, the same issues kept coming up as a roadblock for superior outcomes.

The owner

Specifically, the time the owner had to spread across the whole of the business was at the heart of issues related to growing the business.

It was always a variation of a theme about time and productivity:

"I have too much to do."

"If I work on this, then other things suffer."

"I can't hand things off to anyone."

On and on, owners I met with struggled with the resource of time.

As a small business grows, the owner takes on more. It is natural to just do it yourself in the beginning because you are the company. Even when the time has come where staff can be added, it means you, as the owner, are taking on more.

Filling a new position is a great example of how the objective of reducing your work results in more work upfront, and may initially deter an owner from ever getting more help.

1. The work that you eventually want to delegate to the new position still needs to be done.

2a. Now you add the work of filling the position.

2b. Then after completing the hire of a new staff member, you have the work of onboarding the new hire.

3. While you eventually get rid of the work you wanted to delegate and the extra work of hiring and onboarding, you may now have new ongoing work of payroll and staff management.

The business and the owner suffer because there is only a finite amount of time they have and the act of juggling leaves the owner with a growing feeling that they are not giving all areas of business the attention they deserve.

Does this sound like your situation?

How do we solve this problem?

Rather than you go out and laying out some audacious strategic plan, I suggest we start planning your business from the point of the most important and constrained resource there is: You.

APPLYING THE THEORY OF CONSTRAINTS TO PERSONAL PLANNING

You only have so many hours in a day and, more importantly, since you are the business owner, you deserve to have a business that serves you, not the other way around. To solve this problem, I have drawn from the work of Dr. Eliyahu Goldratt, who conceived the "Theory of Constraints" (TOC) in his book "The Goal." His ideas have been improved and adapted by others to supplement operational improvement concepts like lean manufacturing. The same concepts that can be used to improve a manufacturing process can be applied to help improve personal output.

Time Mapping Exercise

Purpose: To design the life of the business owner and align the business strategy with that life.

Expected Result: To create a structure for time management that supports the business and life goals. This map can then be further broken down to monthly and weekly scheduling to create the time for tactical support of the strategic time map.

Let's begin with two key concepts that we will go back to whenever we lose sight of why we got into this business in the first place:

1. The business is here to serve you, not you serve the business. Begging the question: "What do you want you out of the business?"

2. You are the business bottleneck. Productive use of your limited resource of time drives your business.

Time may be a bigger constraint than money

For most small businesses, it is not money that holds the business back but the use of owner's time. This is because one of the biggest resource exchanges an owner can do is changing the time for money. What do I mean by this?

Simple: if an owner can't hire someone to do something because they can't afford the salary, they do it themselves, thereby converting their time to money. Sometimes called sweat equity; this is how much of the initial value is created in a business by the owner doing the work, but when they run out of hours or spend hours on the wrong stuff, the business begins to suffer.

The willingness to sacrifice for the business to succeed turns from a positive trait to a personal curse because sooner or later, you begin to feel burned out and overwhelmed because there is no more time to draw on.

Therefore, if we take the two principles of the business is to be designed to serve your purpose and its key resource constraint is your time, then we need to work within this framework for the best outcome.

In the Theory of Constraints, every process (your business) has a constraint and focusing on improving the constraint until it is no longer the constraint is the most effective way to improved profitability or, in this case, productivity.

The process outlines five focusing steps: Identify, Exploit, Subordinate, Elevate, and Repeat. In the case of time management, we know the constraint—the time you have for the business. Therefore, we don't need to spend effort identifying what is the constraint in the process.

Step One: Exploit

In this step, we look to make quick improvements in your time management. First, by exploring where you currently use your time. Using the Time management worksheet, audit your time use over the past three months. We are going to categorize our time into six categories. When thinking of these categories, also note how you feel about the time spent in those categories. You may find that you really like working on the operations of your business or the reason you got into the business was to work with clients. How you feel about the category should influence the time you spend in the area.

Customer/Sales: This is the time you spend with clients selling or developing relationships. This will include the time that you spend on client work. If you're a designer and are producing content for the client, then the time should be allocated to this category.

Operations: This is the work you need to do to facilitate your business and not only includes processes you need to maintain to get the product out the door but also includes, HR, Payroll, ordering office supplies—anything you need to do to manage the organization's operations.

Strategic: Time spent on the business to grow and improve the enterprise. This includes annual planning, strategic marketing initiatives, and other programs that will take the business to the next level.

Personal Development: What are you doing to be a better person and owner? This should include work you do for professional development, continued education, and personal improvement. IF you want your employees to grow and improve, you need to lead by example.

Staff Development: This is group and personal time solely focused on helping your staff get better at their jobs and move down their chosen career path. Meetings about clients don't count. This is dedicated time to helping your subordinates become better people.

Unaccounted time: This exercise typically results in you determining that you don't know what you're doing with all of your time. Many of us run from one fire and let urgency drive our schedule.

An example audit follows:

CURRENT

	MONTH 1	MONTH 2	MONTH 3	AVERAGE	PERCENT
Customers/Sales	10	20	20	16.7	10%
Operations	30	30	30	30.0	19%
Strategic	10	10	10	10.0	6%
Personal Development	1	1	0	0.7	0%
Staff Development	5	5	5	5.0	3%
UNACCOUNTED TIME	104	94	95	97.7	61%
HOURS WORKED	160	160	160	160.0	

This is your current state. We are going to next focus on an ideal future state. This is where you, as the owner, begin to model how you want your time to be spent. I guarantee that if you fix an ideal state and work to it, your business will become far more effective because its leader and the most influential employee will be focused on what matters.

Things to keep in mind:

Put your time where you like to work.

When you find that you're "stuck" because you would like to spend more time in one category but can't because you have obligations in categories you dislike, then start a list of the items you like and dislike in the lower order category and assign hours to them.

You must put time into personal development. You deserve it, and you and your business will benefit from your personal improvement.

If you don't have employees, staff development is not reverent. If you do have employees, then you need to allocate time. You will get more work and commitment for the time you put into this category than you ever would from raises and bonuses. This also becomes critical in company growth through staff development.

Build out your ideal future state on the worksheet to suit how you would like your time to be spent.

Step 1: Plan Future State - Exploit

FUTURE	PERCENT	HOURS LOCATION	WEEKLY
Customers/Sales	40%	64	16
Operations	40%	64	16
Strategic	10%	16	4
Personal Development	5%	8	2
Staff Development	5%	8	2
Other	0%	0	0
TOTAL	100%		
HOURS WORKED	160		

Compare current state and future state to see the disparity between the two and where the work needs to be done to shift to a more proactive state. Don't expect that this will happen overnight. Some of the items could take years to get off your place but before you jump out a window, keep this in mind: without this level of planning we are doing now, the things you hate will always be there for you to do. Today's planning will eventually deliver you the freedom you need.

Step Two: Subordinate

In this step, we are going to review your business and ensure that it is aligned and supports the needs of the constraint (Your Time). As we move into actual business planning, it will be subordinate to your time allotments and when evaluating future initiatives, your time will govern how the business is to grow and operate.

Subordinate

The first step in subordinating your business to your schedule is to schedule one hour a week on your calendar as a recurring event called schedule block. Select a time where you can think strategic, and it won't conflict with other work. It could be early Monday, last things of Friday or a Sunday evening. Whatever works for you to have as a scheduling habit.

Using your future state, begin by scheduling in the hours for the next three months for personal development, stave development operations, and finally sales and customers.

Let's use personal development, for example. Now it is scheduled on your calendar, an appointment with yourself. If you are wondering, "What am I going to do with that time?" make a note on your calendar that the time is to be used to understand what you seek in personal development and find resources. Having the white space in your schedule to think deeply about what you need will give you the opportunity to figure it out; have the time to do the research to eventually fill the time with the classes of activities you want to pursue. The same thing goes for staff development. Schedule the time and begin with figuring out what the future looks like. Schedule the time with an employee. Use the first meeting just to discuss with them where they would like to be in the firm or in their career in a few years. This incremental work will inspire you to fill in the blanks and set the intention for a more positive purposeful use of time in your schedule and organization.

Make sure that the areas that typically get pushed back get firm times on your schedule and are respected. These are typically personal and staff development and strategic, some of the most effective areas of work to strengthen a business and help it grow.

You will need to reconcile the current and ideal state at this point. What I mean by this is, you may have work that you don't like to do in your current state that in your ideal state is not yours to do. The reality is, it still needs to be done, so schedule it now but note that this needs to become part of your strategic or staff development.

Step Three: Elevate

As you consider further actions and plans for the business, do so with the intent to mitigate your time from being the constraint on your business. This can be done by introducing and working on plans that build staff and staff skills to allow you to delegate more of your duties as well as work to move those duties you find unfavorable to others so that your work is not work.

Elevation Method:

Step one: Identifying Work Types

Identify the work you enjoy and the amount of time you <u>would like</u> to spend doing it.

If you like to sell, then that's great; determine how much of your time you want to be spending developing customers.

Categorizing your work:

- Stuff I like to do: This is stuff that got you to go out on your own in the first place. You are good at it and enjoy it. You deserve to keep doing this work.

- Stuff I need to do: This category can be tricky. There are likely things you need to do and will always have to do even if you don't like to do them, like making certain decisions, hiring, and firing. There are also items that you think you must do, but they can go in the next category.

- Stuff I do, but I want someone else to do: This is a toxic category that steals our joy. We need to take inventory here and work to develop our organization to get rid of this category.

Sometimes we are doing things because we just should stay in the early days doing payroll but over time, we can work to actively reduce the items we list here. Worse still is items we are not good at, don't want to do but are afraid to let another do. Besides you know you are not doing them well, and someone else may be really good at doing this work.

- Important but not urgent: Here is the true tragedy in action. You have something you know will be great for you and your business, but you don't have the time to get it done. You know it's important, but there is always something that takes precedence. We will make sure that you set aside the time to do this work, literally scheduling time with yourself to do this.

- Personal Development: This is another category you need to dedicate time to on a regular basis. Reading books like this, going to seminars, working with a coach all help you to be a better person and deliver better results to your team and clients. Dedicating time to this type of work also is a demonstration to your team that personal development is important to you. You lead by example and give your team the time to develop personally and have the expectation that they will work to grow.

If you had these skills, you would not be feeling the way you do and need this help. The great thing is that this is teachable. You will learn the methods and then adopt the habits; furthermore, we will put in place the systems that get your team (if you have one) to do the same and as they grow, you will then have the certainty that they can handle the more complex and sensitive items on your list.

Delegation is our friend

The items that we don't like to do—these are going to get delegated over time. We just might not be comfortable delegating at this point or don't have the person to delegate to identified or trained. This should inform our strategic and staff development getting options in place so that we can continue to elevate and free up more of your time.

VIRTUAL ASSISTANT

Look at using virtual assistance to augment your capabilities.

One shot Deals

There are several websites such as uptake.com that provide venues for you to source one-time virtual workers for specific tasks.

Domain Specific Knowledge

Look to establish relationships with industry experts that you can call on when needed. This is helpful for getting advanced work done on programs that you have basic knowledge of but will occasionally need someone that can set up templates or advanced features as needed.

Full or Part Time Dedicated Assistant

Many soloprenuers work with a part time assistant that helps with scheduling and routine tasks. With today's technology, you can work with someone, and they can be anywhere in the world. Just because your current assistant wants to move to Spain does not mean that you need to find a new assistant; why not work out a virtual assistant position for them?

Training for delegation

Here is a process for training and delegating repetitive computer tasks (this is particularly useful for delegating to a virtual assistant where it is unlikely for you to do face-to-face training):

1. Get a screen capture software like Camtasia or screen flow.

2. Record yourself doing the task on your computer.

3. Edit the recording to add text and steps to make it easier for the viewer to do the task.

4. Have the person you're delegating use your video to do the task. Make sure that you're around for the time they do the task the first time to answer questions.

5. Review with them any added information they may require completing the task to your liking. Add that material into the video.

Here is the nice thing about this process: the person now responsible for the work has a video to refresh them next time they do the task. You have the video to train the next person you might delegate the task to if the current person leaves. Doing this for all computer related tasks in your business will create an awesome training library that will improve your staff development and onboarding.

The Parking Garage

While building the time map, it will be inevitable that you will have to cut out things from your schedule. It is important for your mental health to process these items; otherwise, you will subconsciously continue to carry the burden of them.

As you build your time map, the initiatives that you must postpone go on a list we call the parking garage.

You give yourself permission to park the idea or work here to be dealt with later. This is a conscious process and an agreement with yourself that you will come back to the list later and review it, and when reevaluating your best use of time later, you will review this list and then determine if your priorities have changed or the item no longer is relevant to your business.

I have found by using this process, I have more energy and better focus to complete the items that are part of the time map and therefore get through them and find within a quarter, I can go back to the garage and look to pull out some of those projects that there was not enough time to complete earlier.

The reality is that while you now have portions of your calendar blocked off and have guidelines for generally how your time is to be spent, you will have days or weeks where there are too many things to get done. At any time where you begin to feel overwhelmed, go to the Big three.

THE BIG THREE

I am not sure who originated this idea, and I have heard it from several sources and think that it is a simple and effective way to make the most of each day.

Identify the three things that would make your day complete and considered by you to be a productive day. That is your to-do list for the day. Anything that comes up as urgent should be weighed against your planned list. If this unplanned item that has popped up is not bigger, better, or more urgent than your top three for the day, then it gets put on the list to be done some other day.

Getting your top three done will make your productivity soar. Make a personal commitment that you will get at least one done and strive to get the three done—given you have the time.

Schedule time blocks on your calendar for those top three just as you would a customer meeting. Honor the time commitment the same way you would an appointment with your best customer.

Remember, when you are contacted with something new from a client that they are looking for, you to give them a time when you will complete a task, not drop everything to do it. Rather than moving your time that you have scheduled for the big meaningful items to do work sooner for a client, just schedule around those times. Your client will tell you if it is needed sooner.

How powerful is this? If you work 48 weeks per year and five days each of those weeks and only achieve on average 1.5 of your top three each day, you will get 360 things done. Important, meaningful things.

If you are a writer and the task is writing 2,000 words in those days, that is 720,000 words or 6.8 books a year.

The daily big three should be fed from your time map and essentially are the smaller objectives that you need to get done that build to your bigger goals that you are developing in your strategic and personal development time.

BUSINESS PLAN

From your personal plan, you can now build the organizational plan. With an eye to your time map, you can align your business plan to the map to further subordinate the business to your constraint of time and then focus on elevating the time constraint bottleneck by having your business plans support that need.

You are also in a better place now because you have financial command or are on your way to having financial commence and can align your plan with measurable numbers that you know will set the course for your business along with a realistic understanding of what you can do with the capital you have on hand.

Having gone through the time mapping exercise, you should be in a better frame of mind to respect the time you should allocate supporting your existing business operations and grow them in the coming year. You and your team's time should become the constraint to the overall business plan

We are going to keep this simple; if we can't fit the business plan to **one page**, it is likely too complicated and convoluted to execute. It is my view that before plowing into a new venture or setting the goals for an organization to achieve for the coming year, you need to be confident that the scope of the plan is within your constraints of time and money.

The business plan has three sections:

- Purpose
- Goal

◆ Strategies

Purpose: This is a simple one or two sentence explanation of why you do what you do and who you do it for. It is at the top to help remind everyone why the business exists. This is extremely important if you are the entire staff, as this document will act as a grounding mechanism when you get distracted of frazzled.

Goal: You can have more than one goal or your goal can be a combination of objectives to better describe the result you seek. Seeing as your business is about you generating a profit, having the goal be focused on a financial result is appropriate—something like "Our Goal is to increase sales by 20% and finish the year with $300,000 in sales with a Gross Margin percentage of 30% and an EBITDA of 15%." Another example would be simpler—the goal for [year] is to have an income of $75,000 in salary and distributions.

Strategy: This section is where you outline key initiatives that support your goal. I won't go into detail as to how to develop strategy, as there are dozens of good books on the subject. I would caution that if your business is a small one with the primary focus of providing you purpose and an income, then that remains the primary source of inspiration for your strategy.

Not sure what your strategy is? Then it may be a good idea to revisit your time map and front load your schedule with some time to get focused on your strategy.

For each strategy, do the following:

Describe the Strategy: Describing the outcome of the strategy with a measurable outcome: "Acme will grow its design services in the Midwest by 10%" or better still, "Acme will increase design services sales by $15,000 by increasing the number of customers it sells design services to in the Midwest."

Expected Result: Why are you doing this? Quantify the results of the strategy when it is successful. For example, if your design sales were $150,000 last year, your expectation is $165,000 in sales, and the average margin on Design sales is 50%, you will have $7,500 in gross profit. We now know that this strategy is projected to contribute 25% of the goal.

Capital: What capital is required to achieve this goal? While many companies set an ambitious sales goal, they end up failing because they never looked at what the cost to support that growth would be. In the sales trough and working capital section, we will dive deeper into how to figure out the costs of different strategies. The takeaway is: quantify what is needed from a cash perspective to make this goal happen. Initially, this could be done on a scratch pad to sum up your estimates, or you can go further and develop detailed budgets. Either way, by determining the cost in dollars, we can now also determine a project's return.

You don't want to go after a project that will result in you spending more money than it will eventually deliver, and you also want to understand how an investment of time and money today can provide future returns that are recurring. To do so, we need to begin to structure your strategies in a way that you can go back later and evaluate the results to help you in future planning.

Time: How much of your staff and your time needs to be dedicated to the strategy. Was this accounted for in your Time Map, or in others? If it has not been, then how is it going to get done? The process of subordinating your business plan to your time plan will typically result in you having to make tradeoffs. Doing this now rather than after you have put in half measures on two initiatives and then one or both having to be abandoned is a far better process for you and your business.

Your business plan becomes a simple working document that keeps you on task. Below is an example of a one-page business plan for an independent publisher/novelist. By having a succinct business plan, you can then convert this to a JPG and create lock screens, desktops, and screensavers so you can see your plan on all your devices.

Purpose:
To pursue my dream of writing novels and living on the earnings from my writing.

Goal:
To have $45,000 (run rate of $75,000) in sales by year end income coming from my existing book and two new books.

Strategies
Launch Novel Two in a new genre of Westerns with an annual sales rate of $25,000; launch by June 30.

Launch Novel Three in Romance with annual sales of $25,000; launch by September 30.

Hire developmental editor for both books to improve novel structure. Estimated cost $1,800 per book.

TAXES

THIS SECTION IS by no means a comprehensive guide to taxation but rather designed to cover some of the common issues that business owners face when starting up on their own and not having the experience or the cash to hire an advisor.

Income Tax

You would have a reportable tax situation if you earned more than $400 as a self-employed person. If you are doing consulting, independent contracting, or selling items online (including digital books), expect a 1099 to be filed with the IRS by the person or company paying you. Eventually, this will be flagged, and if you do not report the associated income and pay the appropriate taxes, you will be getting a letter from the IRS.

Four hundred dollars in revenue is a very low bar to clear and means that you have two obligations; one is to file a return (either personal or a business return), and there are additional taxes due associated with self-employment.

The income tax obligation will be based on your income tax bracket and how you have structured your company. If you are not incorporated, you will report the income on your personal income tax forms. If you have an LLC or LLP, then you will have to pay income tax and self-employment tax on all your profit.

If you are set up as a corporation, then your income tax payments depend on the C or S chapter classification of your company.

If your business is a C corp, then the company pays income tax on profits. You would pay additional income tax on dividends paid to you, resulting in double taxation.

If the business is a subchapter S, then you pay income tax on the profits of the business at your tax rate as well as paying income tax on any salary you draw. This structure is beneficial, as you can set your salary and have a w-2 reporting of income with payment of the associated payroll taxes and no self-employment tax.

Self-Employment Tax

Self-employment tax covers contributions for Medicare and social security. If you are set up as a corporation, then you can pay yourself a salary and along with that salary, pay the associated payroll taxes and Medicare and social security taxes. However, if you are set up as an LLC, you're not paid a salary per se, but take distributions of profits and all profits, regardless of coming out of the business to you or staying in as retained earnings, get taxed.

Quarterly Tax Assessment

Every quarter, you need to estimate the tax liability on the profits in your business. You need to make quarterly payments to state and federal tax collectors to steer clear of penalties and interest. This is one area that can end up surprising new business owners, as their past experiences with income tax have been as a W-2 employee where there is tax withholding for each pay period.

Sales Tax Resale & Retail

Most states, many counties, and municipalities have sales tax provisions where the retailer is required to collect a tax and then report and pay those taxes.

If you are planning to sell as a retailer or a reseller, you will usually need to register for collecting and paying sales tax along with registering for a resales sales tax exemption certificate

FINANCIAL MODELING

FINANCIAL MODELING IS VERY helpful when developing complex businesses or testing out market concepts. In the financial command section, we discussed the use of the 52-week cash flow as a tool for planning and creation of a model for your personal use and as a way to crawl before you walk in modeling. Following are some descriptions of types of financial models and some ideas on how to use them.

If you are looking to raise money or developing a business that has some complexity and feel that this type of excel work is too much for you, I suggest seeking out the help of an MBA student. You can reach out to local business schools nearby to help you do this work.

LOW BASE AND OPTIMISTIC CASES

This is the traditional modeling you will see for a business plan you present a five-year model that shows three scenarios of your business. The model should include an income statement, balance sheet, and cash flow section to demonstrate the effects on the business. Next, you create a low performance, base performance, and finally an optimistic performance case to provide investment cases with a range of outcomes where you can obtain data for analysis of the investment performance. *Go to this link to access the three-case model for all three cases.*

Assumptions

There will be a range of assumptions that should be called out as assumptions. The three cases should have clarity as to changes in assumptions that cause the three different outcomes. It is also helpful if your model has been designed in such a way as assumption variables can be changed and the impact seen within the models. The more you make variables adjustable, the easier it will be for you to test assumption question that comes from you or potential investors. Having the ability to play with variables and see how they impact outcome will get you more comfortable with your plan.

Outcomes Matrix

In an investment case, most models are designed to determine an exit valuation that drives a final internal rate of return. Although all based on assumptions, this provides potential investors with a way to gauge the risk you are presenting in the investment. Here, there will be another layer of assumptions as to what type of multiple there will be on the sale of the business when it is sold.

	EXIT			
MULTIPLE		5		
ENTERPRISE VALUE (EBITDA Multiple + Cash)		$26,880,989		
FEES 4%		$768,965		
DEBT		0		
VALUE TO SHAREHOLDERS		$26,112,023		
MANAGEMENT		1,305,601		
PRINCIPALS		$4,177,924		
Principal Incentive	2%	$522,240		
			COC	IRR
INVESTORS	77%	$20,106,258	2.35	19%
ROUND 1	9%	$2,351,173	3.39	28%
ROUND 2	68%	$17,755,085	2.26	18%

You should use these same tools to evaluate big or complex decisions you make about your business.

While a three-scenario situation is helpful to see the range I have developed and promote the use of multi-variant randomized models to test business plans, what follows is some history on randomizing models and why they are a fantastic risk evaluation tool.

This level of planning and budgeting in a multiple case scenario is great and certainly gets you to understand the risks of your plan. It provides only three outcome "snapshots". Much of today's investment decisions are made on three-case models, but where these models or sales plans fail is: they are built on your bias and assumption that there are few outcomes rather than infinite outcomes. What I will cover next is complex, but I guarantee if you adopt the methods, you will be successful in raising money and running your venture because you will set yourself apart by being one of the select few that embrace uncertainty because you think in terms of probabilities of outcomes.

Let's begin with some basics to set the stage for Multi-Variant Monte Carlo Simulation.

You may be familiar with the bell curve or a normal distribution. Below is a normal distribution of the outcome of rolling two die. Along with probabilities of a number coming up (i.e., seven =.167, 2=.028). Normal

distributions are a powerful model of potential outcomes and are built using the mean (average) of the outcomes and the standard deviation. The next Figure shows a full representation of the standard normal distribution.

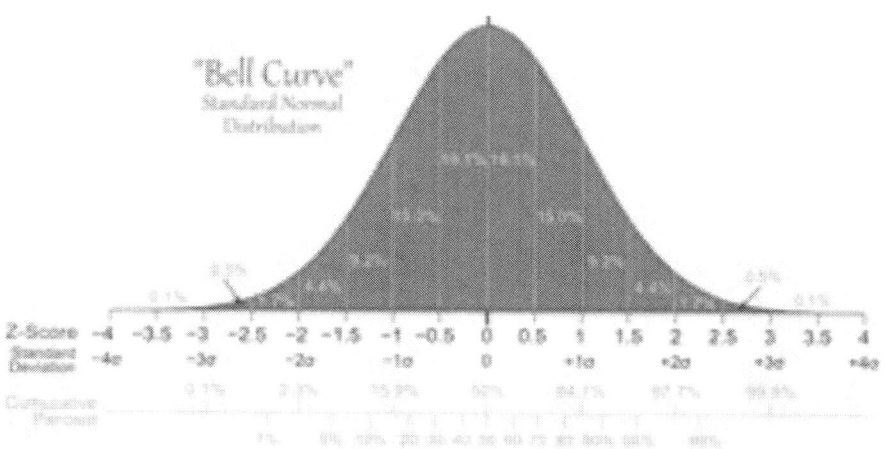

So how can this be important to understanding risk and starting a new business?

As we discussed in the risk section, on average, the US GDP is 3.5% but historically has a range of -9.5% to 16.5%. If your model is based on 3.5% growth, you would be correct to project that because of the average, but the reality is that there is year to year variation that impacts sales based on the economy. So what would be more accurate?

A. A model that depicts a low, middle, and high growth rate.

B. A model that depicts an independent growth rate across a range each year.

C. A model the depicts an independent growth rate but also influences that rate by a secondary variable of the overall economy.

Let's compare:

to keep things simple lets say the business model has these assumptions we will begin year 0 with one million dollars in sales. We will model three cases a low at 3% a base at 5% and a high case at 10%. The model for revenue would look like this.

Three Case Model Assumptions:

	Low	Base	High
Planned Growth	3.00%	5.00%	10.00%

Results:

	YEAR 0	YEAR 1	YEAR 2	YEAR 3	YEAR 4	YEAR 5	GROWTH
LOW	$1,000,000	$1,030,000	$1,060,900	$1,092,727	$1,125,509	$1,159,274	15.9%
BASE	$1,000,000	$1,050,000	$1,102,500	$1,157,625	$1,215,506	$1,276,282	27.6%
HIGH	$1,000,000	$1,100,000	$1,210,000	$1,331,000	$1,464,100	$1,610,510	61.1%

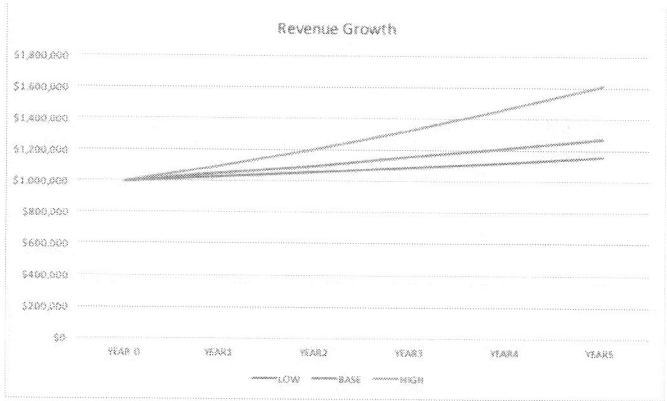

A solid three case model to build your business plan around.

Of course, the more variation we can build into the model, the better so let's instead run three simulations again starting year 0 with one million dollars then each year generating a random growth number using the assumptions that the general economy will have a mean of 3.5% and a standard deviation of 6.5% and we will add our growth of 1.5% mean and 1% standard deviation.

Assumptions:

	Mean	STD Dev
Growth Initiatives	1.50%	1%
General Economy	3.50%	6.50%

Results:

	YEAR 0	YEAR 1	YEAR 2	YEAR 3	YEAR 4	YEAR 5	GROWTH
LOW	$1,000,000	$1,030,000	$1,060,900	$1,092,727	$1,125,509	$1,159,274	15.9%
BASE	$1,000,000	$1,050,000	$1,102,500	$1,157,625	$1,215,506	$1,276,282	27.6%
HIGH	$1,000,000	$1,100,000	$1,210,000	$1,331,000	$1,464,100	$1,610,510	61.1%
SIM1	$1,000,000	$999,425	$1,086,130	$1,047,468	$1,100,371	$1,139,358	13.9%
SIM2	$1,000,000	$1,017,891	$974,151	$1,123,220	$1,176,621	$1,132,942	13.3%
SIM3	$1,000,000	$1,136,151	$1,217,377	$1,178,934	$1,098,521	$1,234,724	23.5%
SIM Avg	$1,000,000	$1,051,156	$1,092,553	$1,116,541	$1,125,171	$1,169,008	16.9%

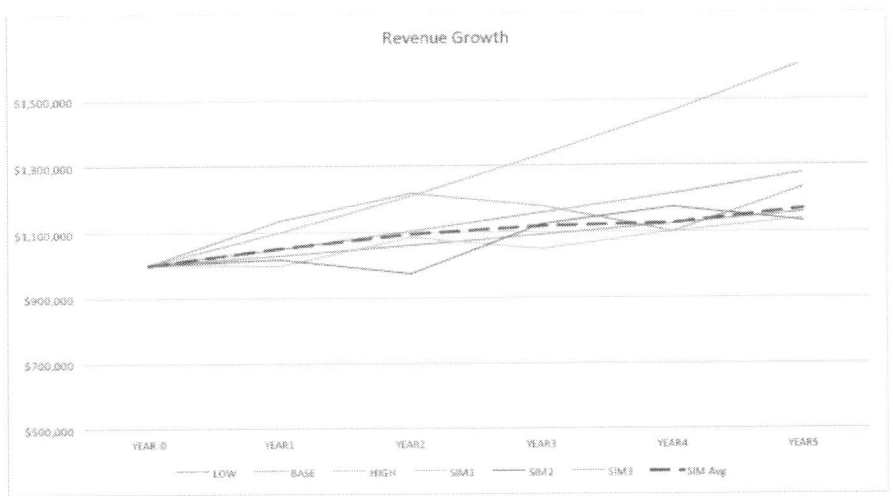

The results are closer to our low case than the base. I know from doing this model I could have had higher results too, the more important feature to me is that the results are not a straight line like a three case. In simulation three our sales drop below one million then go up for two year before another decline - Like real life. Problem is three simulations isn't any more representative of an outcome than our three cases, so how many models do we create to show investors the outcome — three, thirty, thirty thousand?

Here is the solution:

MULTI-VARIANT MODELING

There is a modeling methodology called the Monte Carlo Method. It was developed by a mathematician named Stanislaw Ulam. He was on the Manhattan Project and is considered one of the two developers of the hydrogen bomb. When designing the H-bomb, they were faced with what was known as the neutron diffusion problem. An event with huge randomized events that happened in an instant. Ulam developed a top-secret method code named the Monte Carlo Method to create millions of randomized scenarios, and then use statistics to evaluate probability.

Then applying the **law of large numbers**, a principle of probability according to which the frequencies of events with the same likelihood of occurrence even out, given enough trials or instances. As the **number** of experiments increases, the actual ratio of outcomes will converge on the theoretical, or expected, ratio of outcomes.

In a nutshell, you take a range of variables in your model and let them randomize. Then create thousands of simulations. After creating the simulations(the more the better), you look at the statistics to draw conclusions.

Now we will model the same small business that is doing $1,000,000 a year in sales. The assumptions are far more complex and randomized

Sales: GDP Mean =3.5 STDEV =6.5 and we will randomize and additional 0-4% organic growth

Price Increases: Mean= 1% STDEV =0.5%

Cost Increases (cogs & OpEx) Mean =0.5% STDEV =0.25%

We will run 10,000 iterations of five years of operation.

MC Model Assumptions

MODEL ASSUMPTIONS						
INPUTS			Avg	STDEV	RANDOM
REVENUE	$1,000,000	GDP	3.50%	6.50%	2.15%
EBITDA %	23.0%	Growth	4%		0.7%
EDITDA margin	$230,000	Price improvement	1.0%	0.50%	1.03%
Purchase multiple	6.0x	Cost increase	0.50%	0.25%	0.36%
Transaction value	$1,380,000	COGS	68%		
		TAX	35%		
		Depreciation % sale:	3.0%		

You can look at the MC model file to see the 10,000 iterations and the layout of the simulator. In this simulator every time you hit F9 they recalculate.

To make sense of all the simulations we use a statistics table that consolidates the results within the table you will see little variation in the results change when your recalculate, typically 0.1% change in the average.

Keep in mind this model is not exactly the same as our first model. We added the additional variable of pricing and limited the growth and we did not project extravagant growth.

Below is the simulation results table of the 10,000 samples. The table helps us to understand the results of our simulations.

	SALES	5 year Growth	IRR	MULTIPLE	Y5 EBITDA	EBITDA CAGR
MIN	692,276.6	-6.2%	-11.6%	5.8x	$131,831	-13%
QUART 1	1,175,343	3.5%	9.9%	8.5x	$306,086	7%
MEDIAN	1,296,852	5.9%	13.7%	9.5x	$349,985	11%
QUART 3	1,420,332.37	8.4%	17.7%	10.5x	$395,535	15%
MAX	2,124,937	22%	34.7%	12.8x	$634,790	29%
MEAN	1,305,040	6.1%	13.8%	9.5x	$353,223	11%
STDEV	182,340	3.6%	5.7%	1.24	$66,817	5%
COUNT			10,000			

Immediately we can see that the minimum result was $692,276, meaning after five years business shrunk by 308,000 dollars. Something our three case model would never generate and optimistic business owners typically have a blindspot to negative outcomes.

We can also see that the average and median outcomes are right around 1.3 million dollars in revenue for year five or around 6% growth.

A quick way for assessing outcome probabilities is to take the first and third quartile (quart 1 & 3) to figure out the 50% probability. In this model there is a 50% chance the business will end in year five with 1.17 - 1.43 million in sales.

We can determine with 95% certainty by adding two standard deviations to mean and subtracting two standard deviation to get the results of 1.6 0.93 million dollars.

Here is a chart as to how the sales results are distributed. For those that are visual you can see how of the 10,000 simulations 2179 fall around the median and then instances drop off as we move left and right from the median.

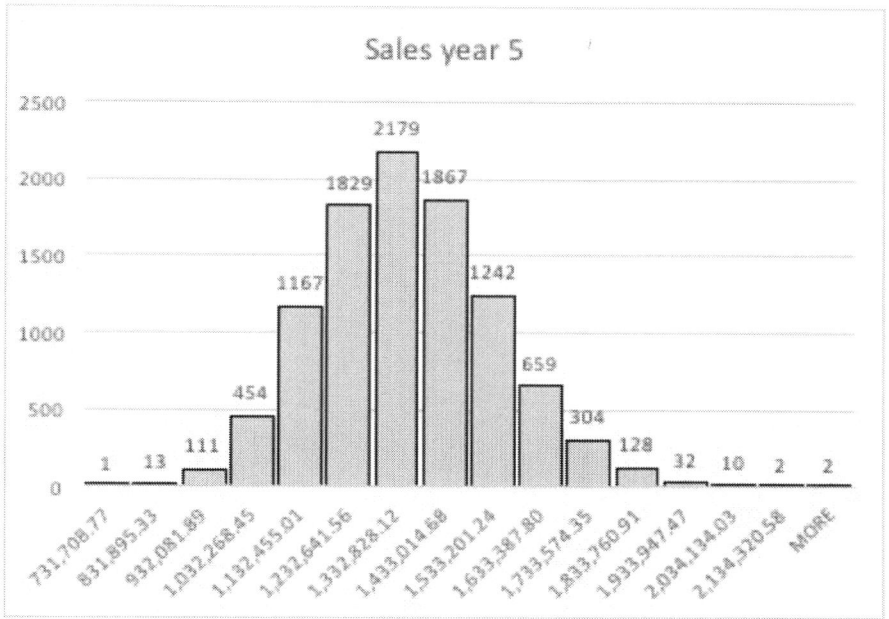

What follows next is the frequency distribution table that was used to build the chart. It give you the numerical results for further analysis.

BINS	FREQUENCY DISTRIBUTION Sales		
	FREQUENCY	CDF	PROB
755,352.49	1	0.00	0.0001
841,910.52	14	0.00	0.0014
928,468.54	98	0.01	0.0098
1,015,026.56	330	0.04	0.033
1,101,584.58	803	0.12	0.0803
1,188,142.61	1373	0.26	0.1373
1,274,700.63	1871	0.45	0.1871
1,361,258.65	1861	0.64	0.1861
1,447,816.67	1562	0.79	0.1562
1,534,374.70	987	0.89	0.0987
1,620,932.72	592	0.95	0.0592
1,707,490.74	280	0.98	0.028
1,794,048.77	149	0.99	0.0149
1,880,606.79	55	1.00	0.0055
1,967,164.81	18	1.00	0.0018
MORE	6	1.00	0.0006
BIN SIZE	10000		1
86,558.02			

The MC model spreadsheet applies this level of analysis though all level of a business finally projecting the potential returns for investors. Also included is a estimate of the chance of a negative return in the case of this model it is 1.42%

Since debt is used to finance the business there is also probabilities projected for default on the debt. The model projects less than 1%.

When looking for investment and faced with investor questions you now have a powerful tool for dealing with hypotheticals that an investor poses. Your fallback answer is alway "We can test that in our model as give you probabilities" This does two things, one is you include the investor in the process of discovering the answer and you show the investor your how you are going to protect their potential investment by using risk assessment and financial modeling. This will go a long way to differentiating you form other seeking investment and help you close your fundraising faster.

I now use this tool to project sales for new projects, potential outcomes from advertising programs; the uses are endless.

This type of modeling is the other end of the spectrum of running a business out of a checkbook with no planning. While I don't see this is for everyone, those that are interested should look at the included dynamic models. If you are intimidated by what is involved in building models like this but feel they will help you in planning your business or raising money, you can always go to your local business school and get an intern to do this work.

WHAT NOW?

I HOPE that you have gotten a few how's out of the book to support your why.

If you are planning to start a venture look to the tools in the financial command and planning section to develop a great ACTIONABLE plan. Don't get lost in the fantasy of planning get a good solid plan, test your assumptions and then take start working the plan.

If you have an operation just try out one of the practices in the book for the next quarter and see the impact it has on your business. Deliberate incremental improvement will have a huge impact on your business. Pick one problem area and get it right.

If you're not sure where to start and feeling overwhelmed then the answer is obvious, begin with personal time management and planning. Getting the leader of the business on the right path will pull the organization along with the leader. This will also help you to get to the point where you can implement some of the ideas, if currently your saying your too busy to do any of this then it's time to evaluate why you're so busy.

Eighty-five percent of US businesses have under five million in revenue, sixty-three percent have less than one million in revenue. Having a small business that supports your lifestyle is a wonderful gift and you should enjoy it, but If you are looking to have a big cash out then I challenge you to set a plan to achieve just that. To make your business one that is an operation that can be sustainable without you and grow it to above that five-million-dollar mark opens doors to a staggering number of firms looking to buy well-built small businesses, you will be able to entice professional buyers with deep pockets (currently 750 billion in private equity money in play) to provide you an exit or growth capital to take the business to the next level.

Finally, please provide feedback. As mentioned earlier If you have additions for the book as well as success stories from implementing these ideas email me at hi@middle-marketplace.com. Those that do provide good ideas I will include them in future updates that will be free of charge to existing readers of the eBook (you will also get credit in the book and paid)

BIBLIOGRAPHY

Elihu Goldratt The Goal

Robert Higgins Analysis For Financial Management

Kraig Kramers CEO Tools

Mike Michalowicz Profit First

Roman Weil Financial Accounting

AFFILIATE LINKS

Throughout this book, I have suggested various products or services to try. Some I have used, or I am currently using; others typically are similar competitive products that I may or may not have used but have included to help you with your research. Whenever possible, I suggest products that have an initial free service or a low initial cost with services that scale with your business. In many cases, the link to the products that I like is an affiliate link. If you are not familiar with an affiliate link, it is a way for a product or service provider to pay the "affiliate" for sending them a prospect. How and what I get paid vary from service to service. I tell you this for a few reasons:

I do include affiliate links in this book.

At times, if you click on a link and then purchase or subscribe to a product, I will get paid a commission. There is no extra cost to you; the provider pays me as part of their promotion and advertising.

The product in this book I promote are all products that I currently or have used in my business and feel they add value; wherever possible, I promote products that have a free feature to help you when you start up.

To expose you to a means of passive income generation that may align with your business. If there are products you typically promote to clients, see if you can establish an affiliate relationship.

In advance, let me thank you for using the link and purchasing one of the products. I am confident if the product is right for your business, you will see the same value and great support that I have and will get a return on your investment.

CURRENT LIST OF FILES AND WORKSHEETS

The files listed are available at https://middle-marketplace.com/bocfiles

You will need to complete a purchase transaction to have access to the files. You will not be charged nor will you need to use a credit card. As an owner of the book you get lifetime access to the files and any updates or additions.

One Page Business Plan

Annual Plan & Budget

52 Week Cash Flow

One Page Business Plan

Annual Plan & Budget

Five Year Financial Model

Dynamic Financial Model

Creating an Exit Strategy

AFTERWORD

If you liked the book please leave a review at Amazon. It's a huge help to me as an author to get a quality review to improve the product in the future and increase sales of my book. Here is one more trick for you authors, Amazon uses reviews in the search algorithm so if you can include some of these words in your review it will increase my book relevance to these search terms. If you find it too hard to drop one or two of these in no sweat, you are already being a huge help just by giving a review.

- Startup
- Small Business
- Entrepreneur
- How to start a business
- How to run a business

If you're an author feel free to swipe this idea to help your book sales and improve search relevance. ;-)

If you didn't like the book I am sorry.

HERE ARE SOME OPTIONS FOR YOU OTHER THAN BOMBING ME WITH A BAD REVIEW.

1. Email me with your ideas so that can improve the book and get them included in future updates. <u>You will get paid $5 so you will get your money back for the book and you will help me and future readers</u>. This is a positive proactive way to make something better rather than a mean-spirited review.

2. If that won't satisfy you, Amazon will refund you what you paid. If you have trouble getting refund, email me and I will write as the author to see about getting you a refund.

ABOUT THE AUTHOR

Joe Solari was born and raised in the Chicago Illinois area Joe attended the School of the Art Institute of Chicago where he was conferred a BFA and later earned a MBA from ChicagoBooth School of Business.

He has owned and operated several businesses over his career including working overseas in Australia for four years and a joint venture in India. He has extensive financing experience for small business covering the spectrum of bootstrapping as well as raising over 21 million dollars in less than 18 months for one start-up.

He currently consults with small businesses owners helping them develop growth strategies to get the business working for them not the other way around.

For More Information

www.middle-marketplace.com

Hi@middle-marketplace.com

Printed in Great Britain
by Amazon